Toward an Islamic Theology of Nonviolence

STUDIES IN VIOLENCE, MIMESIS, AND CULTURE

SERIES EDITOR

William A. Johnsen

The Studies in Violence, Mimesis, and Culture Series examines issues related to the nexus of violence and religion in the genesis and maintenance of culture. It furthers the agenda of the Colloquium on Violence and Religion, an international association that draws inspiration from René Girard's mimetic hypothesis on the relationship between violence and religion, elaborated in a stunning series of books he has written over the last forty years. Readers interested in this area of research can also look to the association's journal, *Contagion: Journal of Violence, Mimesis, and Culture.*

Toward an Islamic Theology of Nonviolence

In Dialogue with René Girard

Adnane Mokrani

Michigan State University Press · *East Lansing*

Michigan State University Press
East Lansing, Michigan 48823-5245

LIBRARY OF CONGRESS CATALOGING-IN-PUBLICATION DATA
Names: Muqrānī, ʻAdnān, author. | Palaver, Wolfgang, 1958– other.
Title: Toward an Islamic theology of nonviolence : in dialogue with René Girard / Adnane Mokrani.
Description: First. | East Lansing : Michigan State University Press, 2022. |
Series: Studies in violence, mimesis, and culture | Includes bibliographical references and index.
Identifiers: LCCN 2021052840 | ISBN 9781611864304 (paperback) |
ISBN 9781609176990 | ISBN 9781628954678 | ISBN 9781628964615
Subjects: LCSH: Nonviolence—Religious aspects—Islam | Violence—Religious aspects—Islam |
Violence in the Qur'an. | Girard, René, 1923–2015. Violence et le sacré.
Classification: LCC BP190.5.V56 M86 2022 | DDC 297.5/697—dc23/eng/20220113
LC record available at https://lccn.loc.gov/2021052840

Cover design by David Drummond, Salamander Design, www.salamanderhill.com.
Cover art: Salaman and Absal repose on the happy isle, folio from a Haft awrang (Seven thrones) by Jami (d. 1492) probably Mashad, Khurasan, Iran, Safavid dynasty, 1556–1565 (ink, opaque watercolour and gold on paper). Bridgeman Images, used with permission.

Visit Michigan State University Press at *www.msupress.org*

To Paolo Dall'Oglio

Contents

ix FOREWORD, *by Wolfgang Palaver*

xix INTRODUCTION. Interpreting Girard's Silence

1 CHAPTER 1. Theory and Principles

43 CHAPTER 2. The Qur'ānic Narratives

73 CHAPTER 3. The Historical Narratives

93 NOTES

107 BIBLIOGRAPHY

115 INDEX

Foreword

Wolfgang Palaver

The French American cultural anthropologist René Girard has claimed a universal significance for his mimetic theory and stated sometimes, too, that it also represents a universal theory of religion. Following the Swiss Jesuit Raymund Schwager who was one of my teachers in Catholic theology in Innsbruck and one of the first theologians who collaborated with Girard, I have focused over many years on the relationship between violence and religion. When suddenly the 9/11 terrorist attacks occurred in 2001, I felt that my research focus would need to shift in light of this event. Islam, for instance, was not a religion that we studied in those days in groups influenced by Girard. A first step was provided by Girard himself when he claimed in an interview two months after the terrorist attacks that they mainly resulted from an increased planetary competition and were not caused by Islam as such.[1] Nevertheless, the question of how Islam may be understood from the viewpoint of mimetic theory has since remained with me and many other scholars dedicated to mimetic theory. There were some Girardians who started to claim that Islam is an archaic religion and is therefore more prone to violence than Christianity because it is rooted, like all early religions, in a scapegoat mechanism. I was not convinced and did not follow this interpretation, even when Girard himself sometimes leaned toward this side of the debate. My first attempt to come to a better understanding of Islam led me to read Mahatma Gandhi who, like Girard, emphasized the importance of nonviolence in our modern world but was also in close contact with many Muslims throughout his life. Without overlooking violent temptations among some Muslims, he recognized Islam as a religion of peace that is not fundamentally different from Christianity or other world religions. According to Gandhi, Islam "is like all other great religions a religion of peace"[2]—all world religions are "equally true and equally imperfect" and "none is superior, none is inferior, to the other."[3] Gandhi focused primarily on the "religion which underlies all religions."[4] In his seminal book *Hind Swaraj* (1909), he summarized this religious core that he discovered in all world religions as follows: "Hinduism, Islamism, Zoroastrianism, Christianity and all other religions teach that we should remain passive about worldly pursuits and active about godly pursuits, that we should set a limit to our worldly ambition, and that our religious ambition should be illimitable. Our activity should be directed into the latter channel."[5] For me, this insight comes very close to the Christian distinction between temporal and eternal goods that becomes highly plausible if it is understood with the help of mimetic theory, because one of the preconditions by which mimetic desire leads to rivalry and violence depends on the objects of our desires. If the object of our desire cannot be divided or enjoyed together, then imitating the longing for such goods will result in rivalry and violence. This is true for many material or worldly objects. Eternal goods differ because their essence does not automatically cause violence, as Augustine, Thomas Aquinas, Dante, or Max Scheler very well understood.[6]

It was such a broader understanding of religion—the holy in distinction from the sacred of early religions—that motivated me to study world religions with the help of mimetic theory. With Richard Schenk, a Catholic theologian who was at that time teaching at the Graduate Theological Union in Berkeley, in 2011 I organized a conference that invited experts of different world religions to discuss the impact of mimetic theory with Girardians.[7] We focused especially on Girard's book *Sacrifice* that showed a certain openness toward Eastern religions as it referred to some parallels between the biblical revelation and similar developments within Buddhism and the Vedānta.[8] Among the experts on world religions, we had an Islamic scholar among us but not yet a Muslim theologian. This changed with two conferences that Sheelah Treflé Hidden, Michael Kirwan, and I organized at the

Heythrop College in London in 2013 and at the University of Innsbruck in 2016.[9] These two meetings included experts in mimetic theory, Islamic scholars, and Muslim theologians and attempted especially to listen to how Muslim scholars view mimetic theory. Adnane Mokrani was one of the Muslim theologians who participated in London as well as in Innsbruck. I knew him already since 2010 when the Focolare movement and my Innsbruck colleague Roman Siebenrock organized a first meeting between Christian and Muslim theologians that has resulted in a still ongoing annual week of dialogue and exchange with international participation. Mokrani's papers that he presented in London and Innsbruck showed clearly that Islam shares important insights with Girard's anthropology and that it is not at all an archaic religion. Bill Johnsen, the editor of this book series, participated in all these conferences and invited Adnane Mokrani to write a book based on his two lectures. I am glad for Bill's invitation and even more so for Adnane's acceptance to write a book that engages with mimetic theory from a Muslim perspective. When I read the final version of this book, I immediately realized what a landmark this book will become for a broader religious reception of mimetic theory as well as for the Christian-Muslim dialogue.

Mokrani's book shows that mimetic theory is not just a Christian anthropology but that it provides a universal theory of religion. At the same time, it encourages scholars of mimetic theory, too, to open themselves to the pluralism of world religions and to leave claims of a Christian superiority behind. With the help of this book, mimetic theory can move closer to Gandhi's thesis about the equality of all religions.

The careful reading of the Qur'ān that Mokrani laid out in this book allows him to show that Islam is not an archaic religion but that, like Judaism and Christianity, it departs from the early sacred. Islam participates in the exodus from archaic religion that I call an "Abrahamic revolution."[10] Mokrani demonstrates in his reading of the story of Abraham's sacrifice in the Qur'ān that "Islam is a post-sacrificial religion par excellence." Girard's most mature reflections on the relationship between archaic religions and the biblical revelation emphasize a paradoxical unity that comprises a discontinuity and a continuity between them.[11] For this reason, Girard emphasizes a transformation of the sacred into the holy and not its separation.[12] A similar understanding of transformation can be discovered in this book where Mokrani claims that the "only meaning of animal sacrifice in the Qur'ānic vision is social solidarity with the poor." Blood sacrifices became a means for human solidarity.

Mokrani's reading of the Qur'ān comes closest to Girard's mimetic anthropology where he focuses on the need to overcome the egoistic self by orienting oneself toward God. He summarizes his interpretation of this Qur'ānic insight in the following way:

> As a monotheistic religion, Islam emphasizes the importance of having God as the only and last "desire." The unification of desires is liberation from all desires, just as the adoration of the One God is liberation from any attachment and idol. On several occasions, the Qur'ān insists on the need to direct desire toward God, as the only finality and satisfaction of human desire.

To orient our desires toward God comes close to Gandhi's understanding of the religion that underlies all religions. Moreover, it finds also an important parallel in Girard's first book, *Mensonge romantique et vérité romanesque*, which carries as its motto a quote from Max Scheler that human beings must choose between God or an idol.[13] The final chapter in Girard's book explains the conversion that enabled the great novelists to overcome their mimetic temptations by letting their prideful egos die.[14] This death of the ego finally allowed them to write their masterpieces. It chimes with insights of Eastern religions and comes very close to Sufism with its emphasis on a purported ḥadīth, "Die before you die," that also aims at the overcoming of a limited and self-centered ego to receive a true self from God. Mokrani rightly claims that the idol as the alternative to God "is, par excellence, the ego." An important chapter takes up the question of Jesus's Crucifixion that is central in Girard's anthropological apology of Christianity and is also a key topic in Christian-Muslim dialogues. Mokrani shows first that there is no Islamic consensus in denying the Crucifixion. Furthermore, he interprets the Cross in line with his emphasis on the overcoming of the egoistic self as a "real symbol" of the "conversion to God." Spiritually it means for him the "conversion within every human being, the death and resurrection of each one." To underline this claim, he refers to the above mentioned ḥadīth and to Sufism. Regarding Jesus, it must be underlined, too, that Mokrani states that an Islamic theology of nonviolence "cannot ignore Jesus as a source of inspiration."

Mokrani's book is, however, not only an essay that expresses its view of mimetic theory; it also offers a helpful guide to overcome a simple view of Islam that often equates this religion with violence. It engages with ambivalent passages in the Qur'ān like the story of "Moses and the Violent Saint" and throws a light on the history of Islam to understand the challenges it met regarding violence. Mokrani does not shy away from ethical dilemmas like the violent punishment of the Jewish tribe of Banū Qurayẓa and explains that it cannot be understood as a prophetic model for today but only as the "ethical choice in its historical context." This, however, does not mean that Mokrani justifies Islamic history without any reservations. To the contrary, he states that some historical narratives contradict the Qur'ānic message of mercy and peace and support an expansionist and imperialist jihadism. Such a view has turned conquests that were the exceptions into the rule. With the help of Girard, he shows that these conquests often served to overcome internal rivalries by scapegoating an external enemy. He warns his readers that the imperialist temptation is not over. It has become an "imperialism without empire" that inspires some Muslims today but must be overcome because it distorts the basic message of Islam.

In view of the current state of our world, I appreciate the general outreach of this book toward nonviolence most. This is a timely approach that is desperately needed. In this regard it positively complements Girard's anthropology that lacks to some degree a political and activist dimension. Mokrani refers frequently to political dimensions of his understanding of Islam. His reading of the story of "Joseph and His Brothers" underlines, for instance, that forgiveness and nonviolence are no longer part of an individual ethic but have, due to Joseph's role as a leader, a political meaning. This becomes even more explicit in a chapter that shows that the Islamic principle of non-compulsion in religion leads to the conclusion that the believers should manage their affairs through consultation. "Consultation" is, according to Mokrani, "the first social expression of nonviolence and non-compulsion." Without democratic dialogues, tyranny and hypocrisy would prevail.

Part of Mokrani's political focus is a short chapter that introduces the readers into Islamic peace ethics by naming all of the conditions that must be fulfilled to justify responding violently to violence. This Qur'ānic realistic pacifism as he calls it, however, is not Mokrani's final answer. In his concluding chapter, "Modern Challenges," he emphasizes the importance of nonviolence for our world of today. With Ramin Jahanbegloo, an Iranian scholar focusing on nonviolence, Mokrani underlines the "Gandhian moment," which proposes nonviolence as the appropriate way to fight against injustice in the modern world.[15] He introduces Muslim thinkers and activists—such as Abdul Ghaffar Khan, Maulana Abul Kalam Azad, or Asghar Ali Engineer—who were influenced by Gandhi and adopted radical nonviolence. Moreover, he underlines, with the Indian Maulana Wahiduddin Khan, that nonviolence "should never be confused with inaction or passivity."[16] This active understanding of nonviolence concurs fully with Gandhi's concept that insisted how important it is to distinguish it from passivity. Girard remarked regarding Gandhi that he combined the philosophy of Jainism with Christianity and that it was due to the latter that he opted for "political action."[17] Indeed, Gandhi insisted against widespread Christian assumptions that Jesus must be understood as a nonviolent activist. In his book *Satyagraha in South Africa*, he underlines the active nonviolence that he recognized in Jesus Christ: "Jesus Christ indeed has been acclaimed as the prince of passive resisters but I submit in that case passive resistance must mean satyagraha and satyagraha alone."[18] Satyagraha was understood by Gandhi as an active force, as truth- or love-force. Today, most Christians are not surprised to understand Jesus in this active way. They learned it partly from Gandhi. It is, however, also important to remember that Gandhi's collaboration with Muslims in his struggle against discrimination toward Indians in South Africa contributed to his emphasis on active nonviolence, as Gita Dharampal-Frick remarks in her postscript to the German translation of Gandhi's autobiography.[19] With Mokrani's book, we can understand this relation between Islam and Gandhi even better and can hope that it will strengthen efforts toward nonviolence in our world.

Notes

1. Cynthia L. Haven (ed.), *Conversations with René Girard: Prophet of Envy*, Bloomsbury, New York, 2020, pp. 85–90.
2. Mohandas Karamchand Gandhi, *The Collected Works of Mahatma Gandhi. Vol. 33: January–June 1927*, The Publications Division, New Delhi, 1969, p. 357.
3. Mohandas Karamchand Gandhi, *The Collected Works of Mahatma Gandhi. Vol. 64: November 3, 1936–March 14, 1937*, The Publications Division, New Delhi, 1976, p. 420.
4. Mohandas Karamchand Gandhi, *Hind Swaraj and Other Writings*, Cambridge University Press, Cambridge, 1997, p. 41.

5. Ibid., pp. 41–42.

6. Wolfgang Palaver, *René Girard's Mimetic Theory*, Gabriel Borrud (tr.), Studies in Violence, Mimesis, and Culture, Michigan State University Press, East Lansing, 2013, pp. 93–95.

7. Wolfgang Palaver and Richard Schenk, eds., *Mimetic Theory and World Religions*, Studies in Violence, Mimesis, and Culture, Michigan State University Press, East Lansing, 2018.

8. René Girard, *Sacrifice*, Matthew Pattillo and David Dawson (tr.), Breakthroughs in Mimetic Theory, Michigan State University Press, East Lansing, 2011.

9. Michael Kirwan and Ahmad Achtar, eds., *Mimetic Theory and Islam: "The Wound Where Light Enters,"* Palgrave Macmillan, New York, 2019.

10. Wolfgang Palaver, "Monotheism and the Abrahamic Revolution: Moving Out of the Archaic Sacred," in *The Palgrave Handbook of Mimetic Theory and Religion*, James Alison and Wolfgang Palaver (eds.), Palgrave Macmillan US, New York, 2017, pp. 103–109; Wolfgang Palaver, "The Abrahamic Revolution," in *Mimetic Theory and World Religions*, Wolfgang Palaver and Richard Schenk (eds.), Studies in Violence, Mimesis, and Culture, Michigan State University Press, East Lansing, 2018, pp. 259–278.

11. René Girard, *Battling to the End: Conversations with Benoît Chantre*, Mary Baker (tr.), Studies in Violence, Mimesis, and Culture, Michigan State University Press, East Lansing, 2010, xv, 175; René Girard, *The One by Whom Scandal Comes*, M. B. DeBevoise (tr.), Studies in Violence, Mimesis, and Culture, Michigan State University Press, East Lansing, 2014, p. 43.

12. Wolfgang Palaver, *Transforming the Sacred into Saintliness: Reflecting on Violence and Religion with René Girard*, James R. Lewis and Margo Kitts (eds.), Elements in Religion and Violence, Cambridge University Press, Cambridge, 2020.

13. Max Scheler, *On the Eternal in Man*, Bernard Noble (tr.), Harper, New York, 1961, p. 399: "Man believes in either a God or in an idol. There is no third course open!" Cf. René Girard, *Mensonge romantique et vérité romanesque*, Grasset, Paris, 1961. The English translation unfortunately omitted the quote from Scheler: René Girard, *Deceit, Desire and the Novel: Self and Other in Literary Structure*, Yvonne Freccero (tr.), Johns Hopkins University Press, Baltimore, 1966.

14. Girard, *Deceit*, pp. 290–314.

15. Ramin Jahanbegloo, *The Gandhian Moment*, Harvard University Press, Cambridge, MA, 2013.

16. Maulana Wahiduddin Khan, *Non-Violence and Islam*, Goodword Books, New Delhi, 2013, p. 3.

17. René Girard, *Evolution and Conversion: Dialogues on the Origin of Culture, With Pierpaolo Antonello and João Cezar de Castro Rocha*, Continuum, London, 2008, p. 212.

18. Mohandas Karamchand Gandhi, *The Collected Works of Mahatma Gandhi. Vol. 29:*

November 1925–February 1926, The Publications Division, New Delhi, 1968, p. 96.

19. Mohandas Karamchand Gandhi, *Eine Autobiographie oder Die Geschichte meiner Experimente mit der Wahrheit*, Shriman Narayan and Wolfgang Sternstein (eds.), Brigitte Luchesi (tr.), Ausgewählte Werke in 5 Bänden, Wallstein Verlag, Göttingen, 2011, pp. 562–563.

References

Gandhi, Mohandas Karamchand. *The Collected Works of Mahatma Gandhi. Vol. 29: November 1925–February 1926.* New Delhi: The Publications Division, 1968.

———. *The Collected Works of Mahatma Gandhi. Vol. 33: January–June 1927.* New Delhi: The Publications Division, 1969.

———. *The Collected Works of Mahatma Gandhi. Vol. 64: November 3, 1936–March 14, 1937.* New Delhi: The Publications Division, 1976.

———. *Eine Autobiographie oder Die Geschichte meiner Experimente mit der Wahrheit.* Translated by Brigitte Luchesi. Ausgewählte Werke in 5 Bänden 1. Edited by Shriman Narayan and Wolfgang Sternstein. Göttingen: Wallstein Verlag, 2011.

———. *Hind Swaraj and Other Writings.* Cambridge: Cambridge University Press, 1997.

Girard, René. *Battling to the End: Conversations with Benoît Chantre.* Translated by Mary Baker. Studies in Violence, Mimesis, and Culture. East Lansing: Michigan State University Press, 2010.

———. *Deceit, Desire and the Novel: Self and Other in Literary Structure.* Translated by Yvonne Freccero. Baltimore: Johns Hopkins University Press, 1966.

———. *Evolution and Conversion: Dialogues on the Origin of Culture. With Pierpaolo Antonello and João Cezar de Castro Rocha.* London: Continuum, 2008.

———. *Mensonge romantique et vérité romanesque.* Paris: Grasset, 1961.

———. *The One by Whom Scandal Comes.* Translated by M. B. DeBevoise. Studies in Violence, Mimesis, and Culture. East Lansing: Michigan State University Press, 2014.

———. *Sacrifice.* Translated by Matthew Pattillo and David Dawson. Breakthroughs in Mimetic Theory. East Lansing: Michigan State University Press, 2011.

Haven, Cynthia L. (ed.), *Conversations with René Girard: Prophet of Envy.* New York: Bloomsbury, 2020.

Jahanbegloo, Ramin. *The Gandhian Moment.* Cambridge, MA: Harvard University Press, 2013.

Khan, Maulana Wahiduddin. *Non-Violence and Islam.* New Delhi: Goodword Books, 2013.

Kirwan, Michael, and Ahmad Achtar, eds. *Mimetic Theory and Islam: "The Wound Where Light Enters."* New York: Palgrave Macmillan, 2019.

Palaver, Wolfgang. "The Abrahamic Revolution." *Mimetic Theory and World Religions*, edited by Wolfgang Palaver and Richard Schenk, pp. 259–278. Studies in Violence, Mimesis, and Culture. East Lansing: Michigan State University Press, 2018.

———. "Monotheism and the Abrahamic Revolution: Moving Out of the Archaic Sacred." *The Palgrave Handbook of Mimetic Theory and Religion*, edited by James Alison and Wolfgang Palaver, pp. 103–109. New York: Palgrave Macmillan US, 2017.

———. *René Girard's Mimetic Theory*. Translated by Gabriel Borrud. Studies in Violence, Mimesis, and Culture. East Lansing: Michigan State University Press, 2013.

———. *Transforming the Sacred into Saintliness: Reflecting on Violence and Religion with René Girard*. Edited by James R. Lewis and Margo Kitts. Elements in Religion and Violence. Cambridge: Cambridge University Press, 2020.

Palaver, Wolfgang, and Richard Schenk, eds. *Mimetic Theory and World Religions*. Studies in Violence, Mimesis, and Culture. East Lansing: Michigan State University Press, 2018.

Scheler, Max. *On the Eternal in Man*. Translated by Bernard Noble. New York: Harper, 1961.

INTRODUCTION

Interpreting Girard's Silence

This research does not offer a general evaluation of René Girard's mimetic theory, which attempts to explain the origin and development of religions; a complex and demanding task that needs more preparation. The goal of this study is rather simple: to discuss Girard's book *I See Satan Fall Like Lightning*,[1] in which the theory is applied to the Hebrew Bible and the New Testament, with a special focus on the Cross. In this book, Girard argues that the role of religion, Judaism and Christianity in particular, is to decrease, if not eradicate, violence. His analysis is profoundly Christian; Jesus Christ is seen as the apex of a long historical journey; in him, the problem of evil has been definitively resolved, in the sense that the Christ model offers a sufficient and complete answer.

According to Girard, myths reverse the truth, treating the innocent as guilty. The Cross, however, denies any mythology, declaring the innocence of the victims. Jesus himself calls the mechanisms of mimetic rivalries, which lead to the scapegoat, "scandal." Girard underlines the break between Christianity and pagan mythology: they are opposite as thesis and antithesis, from which he deduces the absolute "uniqueness" of Christianity,[2] which is presented not only in the Cross but also in other evangelical stories such as the story of the adulterous woman.[3]

The challenge is to guarantee that the Christian "uniqueness" does not turn into a Christian "supremacy," is to go beyond Girard's specific Christian language and see if the principles and values expressed in the mimetic theory can be expressed in non-Christological religious languages, in a potentially universal uniqueness. "As always, his [Jesus] word, dignifies something universally human,"[4] affirmed Girard, who wants to give the Gospel a universal value that goes beyond the confines of Christianity, maintaining, at the same time, the centrality of the Christian language. It is a challenging task, mainly because Girard is very skeptical of pluralistic theologies of religions, seeing in them risks of relativism. This study hopefully could help to overcome this theological problem, that is, the conciliation between uniqueness and universality.

Girard did not deal systematically and profoundly with Islam. Thomas Scheffler well summarizes and evaluates the fragmented allusions to Islam in Girard's books and interviews:

> Girard did not leave us a systematic treatise on Islam. His scattered comments on Islam-related topics are few in number and were (with a few exceptions) mainly published after the terrorist attacks of 11 September 2001, that is, at a rather late phase of Girard's work. In addition, most of these statements were uttered in the context of (shorter or longer) interviews in which Girard focused more on contemporary Islamist radicalism than on Islam in its entirety. Girard himself once explained the relative marginality of Islam in his work by his deficient knowledge of Arabic and by the contradictions between the few French translations of the Qurʾān that were accessible to him.[5]

Although Girard recognizes the limits of his knowledge of Islam, sometimes his "impressions" risk becoming severe and generalized judgments, which somehow reflect the old prejudices about Islam:

> Personally, I have the impression that this religion has used the Bible as a support to rebuild an archaic religion that is more powerful than all the others. It threatens to become an apocalyptic tool, the new face of the escalation to extremes. Even though there are no longer any archaic religions, it is as if a new one had arisen built on the back of the Bible, a

> slightly transformed Bible. It would be an archaic religion strengthened by aspects of the Bible and Christianity. Archaic religion collapsed in the face of Judeo-Christian revelation, but Islam resists. While Christianity eliminates sacrifice wherever it gains a foothold, Islam seems in many respects to situate itself prior to that rejection.[6]

This research opens new windows in dialogue with Girard's thought, showing that Islam is not a neo-archaic religion of sacrifice. In the Qurʾān, as in the Bible, there are the elements necessary to overcome the archaic sacrifice. However, no immunity prevents religions, including Islam and Christianity, from being transformed into "military religions." The significance of mimetic theory lies precisely in its ability to dismantle the theologies of power. This dismantling interests us in this book, not some negative observations on Islam that could hide the relevance of the theory.

The questions in this research include the following: Can we extend the application of the mimetic theory on the Qurʾān? What is the Qurʾānic answer to the burning question of violence? This research is an attempt to fill a gap: interpreting Girard's silence about Islam and developing an Islamic theology of nonviolence, a mystical narrative theology of radical peace. Disarming theology is the first step toward serious reform of religious thought, freeing religion from the temptations of domination and power. A reflection that leads us to redefine religion itself, as a vision and as a mission. A new Islamic theology should be interreligious if it wants to be universal and in continuous dialogue with other theologies, especially the Christian ones.

This book is divided into three chapters: the first one discusses Girard's mimetic theory in light of the Qurʾān, following the Girardian methodology in the study of the Hebrew Bible and the New Testament. This chapter deals with the theoretical part of the Qurʾān, where the principles are expressed directly and conceptually. The second chapter analyzes the narrative part of the Qurʾān, which confirms the theory in a more symbolic language. The separation between theory and narrative is a methodological procedure for clarifying ideas; therefore, we already find narrative hints in the first chapter. The second chapter is dedicated to the Qurʾānic stories more structurally and systematically. The book does not cover all the Qurʾānic narrative; there is still room to add other stories and more details, especially at the comparative level. The third chapter is dedicated to historical narratives, meant as a collective memory, sometimes sacralized and considered part of religion. The third chapter concludes with modernity's challenges, noting modern and contemporary Islamic efforts to develop nonviolent thought and practice.

The mimetic theory has opened my eyes to the more profound and urgent meaning of religion. It allowed me to see religion and Islam differently. Although I have not solved all my problems with the theory, in the sense that I still have some doubts and certain questions to discuss, but what seems to be the core of the theory, that is, the peaceful mission of religion, remains a fundamental achievement. This research tends to explain the questionable points and appreciate and enlarge the most significant part.

Dialogue with René Girard's thought allowed me to develop an Islamic theology of nonviolence, which is still an open construction site. Indeed your criticisms and comments will contribute to making this project more rich and complete. The book's title is inspired by Jacques Dupuis's book *Toward a Christian Theology of Religious Pluralism*.[7] I believe that the theology of religious pluralism has a close relationship with the theology of nonviolence, aiming to make the human being less violent, accepting the diversity of creation at all levels as divine Will and supreme Wisdom. It is also important to reconsider the theological character of Girard's work, even though he preferred not to use theological terms.

This research was not possible without the help and support of my friend Wolfgang Palaver, who introduced me to the world of René Girard. He accepted generously to review the book's draft and wrote the preface. Professor Palaver has invited me to participate in two significant symposiums on "Mimetic Theory and Islam," in London[8] and Innsbruck.[9] The papers I presented in these two occasions have been developed and incorporated into this book. My participation in the cluster "Spiritual, Epistemic and Political Dimensions of Philosophical Dialogue," coordinated by Roman Siebenrock, was a great occasion to discuss some aspects of the book. I sincerely thank the Thiel Foundation for funding the book project. My thanks extend to William A. Johnsen, Trevor Merrill, and Lindy Fishburne for their encouragement and patience. I thank the Institute of Citizenship and Diversity Management at Adyan Foundation (Lebanon), represented by Nayla Tabbara and Ahmed Nagi, for allowing me, through the Religious Social Responsibility for Coexistence and Citizenship project, to meet numerous Muslim researchers from the Arab world and Europe, and to verify and develop with them some ideas from this book.

CHAPTER 1

Theory and Principles

A fundamental element in Girard's thought, which is not a priority in this research, is his critical evaluation of the modern humanities, considered inherently anti-religious.[1] A position that could remind us of Ismāʿīl Rājī al-Fārūqī and his project "the Islamization of knowledge."[2] Girard, in this context, appears to be a supporter of "the Christianization of knowledge."[3] Girard and al-Fārūqī share the radical critique of modernity and the anti-religious ideologies that have influenced the social sciences. We find the same criticism from other Muslim thinkers, such as René Guenon,[4] Seyyed Hossein Nasr,[5] and, differently, Malek Bennabi, who attributes to the "religious idea" a determining role in the equation of civilization.[6]

For Girard, the sacred represents the universal foundation of human culture; it is the heart of the whole social system, the origin, and archaic form of all institutions. In archaic societies, the institutions that the *Lumières* hold to be indispensable for humanity did not exist; in their places, there was nothing but sacrificial rites.[7] For this reason, modern radical exclusion of the sacred is an aggressive and dangerous approach. The mimetic theory is a reconsideration of religion in contemporary knowledge, to prevent the relapse into the evil trap of violence in the name of a reason that despises religion. The mimetic theory offers a reading of the humanities that is modern and, at the same time, considers the social function of religion.

In this context, Girard is the son of the twentieth century, the century that experienced the apex of the secularization of societies and sciences. In the twenty-first century, other risks should be considered: the return of "sacrificial" religions, in forms of violent religious fundamentalisms and populisms, not only in the Islamic context but also on a global level. This risk is higher and more immanent today because it claims to act in the name of religions born as a response to pagan and violent religions, to subsequently reproduce extreme violence in the name of a god who absolutizes violence. The biblical and Qurʾānic God, who exposed the ancient mythical lies, risks being used as a justification for new pagan myths. This risk indeed was always present, but today it has taken on a more dangerous dimension.

We note here that the sacred, according to Girard, is the sacrificial religion, based on the collective murder of the innocent. Judaism and Christianity are "anti-religions" in this sense. They represent the exit from the satanic religion toward a "religion," if we keep the term "religion," which defends the innocent and reveals the mechanism of mimetic sacrifice. They are the foundation of critical ethical consciousness against the unconscious crowd ruled by Satan. Islam is part of this "anti-religious" line in the sense of "anti-pagan."

Even though Islam is a non-sacrificial and non-sacerdotal religion, the mosque's position in the history of Islamic institutions confirms Girard's theory on the religious origin of culture. The Islamic institution par excellence is the mosque, which is at the physical and symbolic center of the city, the mother of all institutions. It is an institution based on non-sacrificial prayer, like the post-Templar Jewish one. Jewish prayer has maintained a messianic sacrificial horizon, hoping to return to the priestly sacrificial form with the reconstruction of the Temple. On the other hand, Christianity has maintained the sacrificial form but with an anti-sacrificial and anti-pagan spirit, where the great Sacrifice has abolished all sacrifices. This transition from institutional centralism to institutional specialization is a well-known phenomenon in the history of religions and civilizations, accompanied by a similar transition in the field of human knowledge. Girard is not the only one to affirm the religious origin of the institutions. His criticism is rather directed to the presumptuous claim of a total break with the religious past, without preserving the "antibodies" against violence produced by anti-sacrificial religions.

The passage from sacrificial and mythical religions to non-sacrificial and anti-mythical religions, from an unconscious and violent religiosity to a critical and ethical religiosity, must not lead to a Manichean evolutionary vision; because these two tendencies have always coexisted, before the Abrahamic religions and after them, inside and outside them. It is a tension that goes beyond any religious classification. For this reason, the Qurʾān, like the Bible, insists that critical and prophetic conscience already existed from the beginning of human history, knowing that prophethood and sainthood have a universal character. Faith in the one God, with all its ethical implications, precedes or at least accompanies sacrificial religion. This ethical faith, contrary to sacrificial wickedness, is well-rooted in human nature, even when sacrificial religions were prevalent. The Scriptures have always represented a parallel "history," an unofficial narrative of the world, which is not written by the powerful and their courts, despite continuing efforts to master and reinterpret this narrative.

Regardless of these Islamic theological considerations, it is difficult to affirm with certainty that human consciousness is an irreversible historical development away from the sacrificial religions called pagan. Indeed, it cannot be confirmed that these religions lacked the ethical sense of justice, even in primitive forms. The Girardian judgment seems very severe![8] This tendency to generalize the condemnation of so-called pagan religions exists among many Muslim, Christian, and Jewish theologians. It is the dominant opinion in the Abrahamic faiths to justify spiritual "superiority."

This "modern" evolutionary view, which has historical roots, is confirmed in Girard's classification of societies:[9]

1. Archaic societies that have no other institutions than rites.
2. Ancient and medieval societies, where the rite accompanies and, in some way, doubles all institutions.
3. Modern societies, where the rite is absent or almost absent.

Sacrifice and prohibitions are the mechanisms that help to control everything that appears typically human, that distinguishes humans from animals, which Girard terms "mimetic," or sometimes "hyper-mimetic," desire: our increased capacity for imitation, which leads to rivalry when we imitate the desires of others, and endless conflict when we retaliate against the rivalry and appropriative desire of others.[10] The history of humanity, in this perspective, seems a gradual path toward nonviolence, a way of progressive disarmament. Desire would be increasingly transcendental, gradually overcoming the challenge of violence. It appears that the goal of human history is to erase violence, but what is happening is just the opposite: the increase in violence, a continuous escalation, to the point of threatening the existence of man and the planet. If the goal of religions and particularly Christianity, for Girard, is to reduce violence, could we speak of yet another messianic failure? An idealism that cannot change man's reality and cruelty?[11]

How can we explain this paradox? A possible answer is that the Abrahamic religions, which were born to counter pagan violence, have been absorbed by the same pagan and violent logic. Paganism is now Abrahamic, and the rediscovery of the nonviolent soul of monotheism remains a vital necessity.

Despite that the mimetic desire is not exclusively human, murder, as a result of the violent mimetic desire, is typically human. Ethical conscience is intrinsically linked to the problem of evil and crime. Murder represents a decisive obstacle in the path of maturing a critical moral conscience. In specific religious contexts, this conscience is expressed through prophecy, which for Islam is the sign of God's history. Prophecy, as a universal phenomenon, is a message of humanization and criticism of all human deviation. Despite the difference in language between Girard and the Islamic Tradition, we could say that prophecy and mimetic violence are two conflicting forces in the human soul and society. Prophecy is nothing more than that reparative and reforming voice seeking to help man free himself from his destructive violence. This psychosocial and spiritual vision does not necessarily contradict Girard's evolutionary view, which emphases the dominant tendencies in long historical periods.

If we try to deduce an evolutionary view in the Qur'ān, we probably find the three phases of miracles, as extraordinary phenomena, and proofs of the Prophets' credibility:

1. Miracles are in things, as in the case of Moses par excellence, and before and after him.
2. The miracle is the person of Jesus Christ.
3. The miracle is the idea (or the Spirit), the Qur'ān, confirming the previous miracles.

The evolutionary line in the Qurʾān does not relate directly to the issue of violence or institutional development. However, it could confirm a fundamental Qurʾānic concept: change, including that aimed at reducing violence, starts from the idea that the human being believes in:

> God does not change the condition of a people until they change what is within themselves. (13, 11)[12]

Changing mentalities to stop violence is possible only through dialogue, education, and good example; through the idea that becomes a reality through conviction. Muhammad Iqbal (d. 1938) justified the Islamic doctrine of the conclusion of the revelation in Muḥammad, the Seal of the Prophets, *khātam al-nabiyyīn* (33, 40), that humanity reached a level of maturity and rationality that has allowed more autonomy and independence. In this way, there is no longer a need for a new revelation because humans are potentially more mature.[13] Although, this relative autonomy could be a source of deviation and violence if it is not illuminated by revelation.

Attenuated Demythization

As already mentioned, Islam seems to be the heir of post-Templar Judaism in its prayer centered on the Word of God; Christianity, on the other hand, is more related to Templar Judaism and its sacrifices, with elements of post-Templar Judaism. In this evolutionary perspective, we read the story of Abraham's sacrifice in the Qurʾān, which put an end not only to human sacrifices but also to animal holocausts, which potentially means overcoming the animal sacrifice itself. As many verses show, the only meaning of animal sacrifice in the Qurʾānic vision is social solidarity with the poor. It is in tune with the Qurʾānic vision, based on the idea as a driver of change:

> We have made the animal offerings emblems of God for you. In them is goodness for you. So pronounce God's name upon them as they line up. Then, when they have fallen on their sides, eat of them and feed the contented and the beggar. Thus We have subjected them to you, that you may be thankful. *Neither their flesh, nor their blood, ever reaches God. What reaches Him is the righteousness from you.* Thus He subdued them to you,

> that you may glorify God for guiding you. And give good news to the charitable. (22, 36–37, the emphasis is mine)

The shift from the holocaust (the burned sacrifice) to a mere charitable and social function (the distribution of meat for the poor) could be seen as a "secularization" process, that is, a process of rationalization and functionalization.[14] According to Girard, the rites, due to repetition, are modified and transformed into practices that would appear elaborated by only human reason, but they are derived from religious practices.[15]

In general, Islam and the Abrahamic religions have contributed to the world's demythization and rationalization, and by consequence its gradual secularization. Monotheistic religions have had their part in this long process of secularization, and they are, at the same time, the "victims" of this evolutionary process in its modern stage.

Girard argues that Christianity may appear as an attenuated and softened myth. The attenuation is evident in many late mythical cults.[16] They are therefore not merely myths of death and resurrection, but rather more refined versions of the archaic ones, nevertheless fundamentally similar. What makes Christianity more similar to the myth, and for this very reason, more able to discredit it, is the question of the divinity[17] of the victim, which is absent in the Hebrew Bible and the Qur'ān. Despite the differences, what unites the three Abrahamic religions is precisely the attenuation of the myth, which makes their Scriptures a median way between myth and purely rational discourse.

The opponents of the Prophet Muḥammad have accused the Qur'ān of being a repeated version of the previous Scriptures and ancient myths:

> The unbelievers say: These are nothing but *asāṭīr* (myths, fables, writings, scriptures) of the ancients. (6, 25). See also (8, 31), (16, 24), (23, 83), (25, 5), (27, 68), (46, 17), (68, 15), (83, 13).

The word *asāṭīr* (sing. of *usṭūra*) can be translated in different ways, but what interests us here is that the Prophet's contemporaries saw a continuity between the Qur'ān and previous traditions, especially the Judeo-Christian ones. However, regarding the myths, the Qur'ān still maintains a formal continuity with an essential discontinuity, in the same way, confirmed by Girard for the Bible: The continuity manifests itself primarily in the symbolic language. The myth is a sort of narrative theology, which interprets man and life, giving an existential vision to the whole. The myth marks an entire culture and civilization, offering a hermeneutic horizon. At the same time, the Qurʾān, like the Bible, marks a discontinuity and leads to the myth's delegitimization. If the myth covers and justifies violence, the Qurʾān reveals and denounces it.

Among the common characteristics between the Scriptures and the myths, there is the divine presence that takes different forms, and often intervenes directly and extraordinarily. The Prophets' miracles are part of this dimension. This feature extends to include post-Qurʾānic literature, such as Tradition, prophetic biography, and Sufi hagiographic stories. Despite the importance of the miraculous character of the stories, it is not the central point, but it is only a secondary effect of the divine active presence. For this reason, religion cannot be totally demythologized.

The point of divergence is that the biblical and the Qurʾānic stories are opposed to the decisive question posed by collective violence, its good foundation, and its legitimacy.[18] It is the same question that has always been asked: Would the hero deserve expulsion? "The myth answers at every point 'yes,' and the Bible answers 'no,' 'no,' and 'no.'"[19] The Qurʾān answers in the same manner.

Oedipus's myth ends with an expulsion, which confirms his guilt. The biblical story of Joseph, as the Qurʾānic one, ends with a triumph whose ultimate feature proves his innocence. The systematic nature of the opposition between myth and biblical and Qurʾānic narratives suggests that the latter observe an anti-mythological inspiration. Myths always condemn all isolated and unanimously afflicted victims. They are the work of overexcited crowds unable to know and criticize their tendency to expel and massacre defenseless beings and scapegoats, always keeping them guilty of the same stereotypical crimes.[20] The Qurʾānic logic is to do everything to prevent the explosion of the crisis and its transformation into crime.

The Mimetic Cycle

The mimetic cycle is composed of a tripartite sequence: (1) the crisis; (2) collective violence; and (3) religious epiphany.[21] Girard argues that the cycle is found only partially in the Hebrew Bible, in which there are only the crisis and collective violence, but without the third moment, the religious epiphany or resurrection that reveals the divinity of the victim.[22] It is obvious, in the Hebrew Bible, that victims never rise again: "God is never victimized, nor is the victim divinized."[23] There are always "the mimetic processes of crises and violent expulsions, in mythical as well as in biblical texts."[24] In Christianity, the cycle is *differently* complete, Girard distinguishes between the false resurrections in mythology and the true Resurrection of Jesus. The parallel is quite perfect, but without a full identification.

This opinion, based on the opposition between the Old and the New Testament, is typically Christian. It wants the second to be the fulfillment of the first and sees the resurrection necessarily and only through the divinization of the victim. The resurrection, on the other hand, can have different forms of triumph and recovery. For example, the "resurrection" of the People of Israel was in its salvation from slavery and entry to the Promised Land and then in the Temple's construction, which represents the culmination of this path of restoration and settlement. This path of liberation is already a manifestation of divine glory, God who intervenes in history. The Qur'ān describes this liberating passage in this way:

> We desired to show favor to those who were oppressed on earth, and to make them guides and heirs, and to establish them in the Land, and to show Pharaoh and Hāmān and their armies from them that of which they were apprehensive. (28, 5–6)

It is the victory of the oppressed people against the symbols of the political and military powers of oppression, Pharaoh and Hāmān. These "metaphorical" resurrections are often seen in the Old Testament's patristic reading, as predictions of the Christian Resurrection. The question is: What prevents them from being read, from a non-Christocentric point of view, as "real" resurrections?

After the first liberation, we find other cycles of crisis and resurrection, such as the destruction of the First Temple, the Exile and again the liberation and return to the Promised Land. Even after the destruction of the Second Temple, the messianic expectation remains as a horizon of salvation. The third phase exists but adapted to the monotheistic biblical faith: the nations, *goyim*, against the People, who have a sacerdotal (divine) mission, and which is confirmed and saved every time. The clear difference between mythology and the Bible, as Girard points out, is precisely in calling the victims and oppressors by their names, and the unveiling of the hidden mechanism.

In the Prophets' stories in the Qur'ān, we find the same biblical mechanism as in the story of Joseph. His triumph is resurrection. Sometimes, the third phase takes an eschatological form, in the sense that salvation does not take place in this world but is postponed to the next world, as in the story of "the People of the Trench," *aṣḥāb al-ʿukhdūd*, who were Christian martyrs killed for their faith. The resurrection of the dead represents the final victory of good over evil, "the great triumph," as described in these verses:

> By the sky with the constellations. And by the Promised Day. And by the witness and the witnessed. Destroyed were the People of the Trench. The fire supplied with fuel. While they sat around it. And were witnessing what they did to the believers. They begrudged them only because they believed in God the Almighty, the Praiseworthy. To Whom belongs the sovereignty of the heavens and the earth. God is witness over everything. Those who tempt the believers, men and women, then do not repent; for them is the punishment of Hell; for them is the punishment of Burning. Those who believe and do righteous deeds will have Gardens beneath which rivers flow. *That is the great triumph.* (85, 1–11, the emphasis is mine)

In early Islamic history, Hegira, the emigration of Prophet Muḥammad and his Companions from Macca to Medina, represents a similar experience to the Exodus, a passage from persecution and oppression to liberation and the construction of a state.[25] In Shiism, the eschatological return of al-Mahdī is considered a divine response to the martyrdom of Ḥusayn and the other Imams. Among the Mahdī's names is al-Qā'im, which means "the Risen One." In this way, the mimetic cycle is completed in a messianic time of salvation, where God is more manifest than ever.

The Decalogue

René Girard, in his biblical analysis, uses two types of texts that have to do with mimetic theory: (1) Conceptual or theoretical texts, which deal directly with the subject, in the form of precepts, commandments, or general principles. (2) Narrative texts, such as patriarchs and Prophets' stories in the He-

TABLE 1. The Decalogue between the Pentateuch and the Qur'ān

The Pentateuch	The Qur'ān
You shall have no other gods.	And thy Lord has decreed that you serve none but Him . . . (17, 23)
You shall not prostrate before any graven image.	. . . Shun the filth of idols . . . (22, 30)
You shall not take the name of thy Lord God in vain.	. . . He will call you to account for the making of deliberate oaths . . . (5, 89) Make not Allah by your oaths . . . (2, 224)
Honour thy father and thy mother.	. . . do good to parents. (17, 23)
Thou shalt not kill.	. . . and kill not your people . . . (4, 29)
Thou shalt not commit adultery.	Say to the believing men that they lower their gaze and restrain their sexual passions . . . and say to the believing women that they lower their gaze and restrain their sexual passions . . . (24, 30–31)
Thou shalt not steal.	And (as for) the man and the woman addicted to theft, cut off their hands. (5, 38) . . . a pledge that they . . . will not steal (60, 12)
Thou shalt not bear false witness against thy neighbor.	. . . and shun false words. (22, 30)
Thou shalt not covet another man's property.	And covet not that by which Allah has made some of you excel others. (4, 32). See also (15, 88), (20, 131), (24, 30–31).

brew Bible, or episodes from the life of Jesus in the Gospel. On the Qur'ānic level, the same work can be done by studying these two categories of texts.

Among the theoretical texts analyzed by Girard is the Decalogue,[26] which is a common heritage among the three Abrahamic religions, as demonstrated, in a comparative way, by the Azharite scholar Muhammad Abdullah Draz (d. 1958). The Qur'ān contains all the Mosaic Commandments, except for the observation of Shabbat, which is considered a Jewish peculiarity. The Commandments are scattered throughout the Qur'ānic text.[27]

The tenth commandment is of particular importance to Girard; desiring the things of the other is the source of perpetual wars and the origin of all violence. "If the Decalogue devotes its final commandment to prohibiting desire for whatever belongs to the neighbor, it is because it lucidly recognizes in that desire the key to the violence prohibited in the four commandments that precede it."[28] The Qur'ān also strongly prohibits this selfish desire, called envy and jealousy, in several verses, as it has been mentioned:

> Do not covet what God has given to some of you in preference to others. For men is a share of what they have earned, and for women is a share of what they have earned. And ask God of his bounty. God has knowledge of everything. (4, 32)

> Tell the believing men to restrain their looks, and to guard their privates. That is purer for them. God is cognizant of what they do. And tell the believing women to restrain their looks . . . (24, 30–31)

> Do not extend your glance toward what We have provided certain groups of them as a glitter of the life of this world, so that We may test them thereby. The provision of your Lord is better and more lasting. (20, 131). See also (15, 88).

The heart, *qalb*, in the Qur'ān, is the locus of human conscience; its integrity is a condition of salvation, which implies purity from all diseases that pollute it, mainly from the forbidden desire:

> The Day when neither wealth nor children will help. Except for him who comes to God with a sound heart. (26, 88–89). See also (37, 84).

The prophetic Tradition confirms the priority of the interior life over actions, which their value depends on the intention:

> Deeds must be measured against the intention behind them. Every man gets only what he intends. If he emigrates with the intention to seek God and His Messenger, then his emigration (*hijra*) is to God and His Messenger, but if his emigration is undertaken for the sake of worldly prosperity or in order to marry a wife, then his emigration is for what he has emigrated.[29]

Satan as a Scandal

To better understand what the tenth commandment warns, we need to look Satan in the face. Girard mentions several biblical names of Satan, such as the seducer, the adversary, and the scandal. The role of Satan is the conversion of the mimetic model into an obstacle and rivalry; it is the genesis of the scandal.[30] *Fitna* would be the Qurʾānic approximative equivalent of "scandal," in Girardian terminology. *Fitna* is semantically a complex word. It means "temptation," "trial," "seduction," "torment." The same word means "confusion and ambiguity"; in moments of difficulty or seduction, one loses his or her lucidity and capacity of distinguishing good from evil; it is easier to slip into sin. One of the names of Satan in the Qurʾān is Iblīs, which, especially in the history of creation, is related to confusion; although it could be of non-Arab origin, precisely from the Greek *diabolos*, many commentators of the Qurʾān have linked it to the Arabic etymological root *l.b.s.*, from the words *lubs* and *iltibās*, meaning "confusion and ambiguity." Iblīs is a seducer and tempter because he manages to lie and embellish evil, giving it names of honor. He is able to manipulate and make fun of man, as we will see later in the story of Adam and Eve. The very word *fitna* can mean "discord and conflict." The first civil war in the history of Islam after the death of the Prophet Muḥammad and among his Companions was called the great *fitna*.

In the following list, we see the main attributes and actions of Satan in the Qurʾān, underlining some Arabic terms used in the description:

- Cause of sin (*azalla*, literally, "cause of slipping") (2, 36), (3, 155), (5, 90), (8, 11), (24, 21).
- Cause of enmity and hatred (2, 36), (5, 91).
- Cause of illegal earning (2, 168, 275).
- Cause of war and conflict (2, 208).
- The enemy (2, 168, 208), (6, 142), (7, 22), (12, 5), (17, 53), (28, 15), (35, 6), (36, 60), (43, 62), (18, 50).
- He promises poverty (2, 268).
- The stoned one (3, 36), (15, 17), (16, 98), (81, 25).
- Cause of fear (3, 175).
- Bad companion (4, 38), (43, 36).
- Cause of perdition and error, *ḍalāl* (4, 60, 119).
- He has a weak cunning, *kayd ḍaʿīf* (4, 76).

- Rebel, *marīd, mārid* (4, 117), (22, 3), (37, 7).
- He sells illusions and false promises, *ghurūr* (4, 120), (7, 22), (14, 22), (17, 64), (25, 29), (59, 16).
- Seducer, *zayyana, aghwā, sawwal, amlā* (6, 43), (7, 175), (8, 48), (16, 63), (27, 24), (29, 38), (47, 25).
- Whisperer, *waswasa* (7, 20), (20, 120), (22, 52), (58, 10).
- Cause of forgetfulness (6, 68), (7, 201), (12, 42), (18, 63), (25, 29), (43, 36), (58, 19).
- Cause of scandal, *fitna* (7, 27), (22, 53).
- Cause of separation and division (*nazagha*, literally, "to enter between" or "to separate") (7, 200), (12, 100), (17, 53), (41, 36).
- Cause of waste (17, 27).
- Falsely worshipped (19, 44), (36, 60).
- Cause of imitation of the ancestors (31, 21).
- Cause of fatigue and punishment (38, 41).
- Arrogant and disbeliever (2, 34), (7, 11), (15, 31–32), (17, 61), (18, 50), (26, 95), (38, 74–75).
- *Ṭāghūt* (4, 76), worshipped in the place of God. The word *ṭāghūt* is a complex term, used in the sense of idol and sometimes of Satan. Its root is from the verb *ṭaghā*, which means to transgress, to go beyond the limits, to commit acts of despotism.

As Girard asserts: "The desire of which Jesus speaks is therefore based on imitation, whether of the devil or of God."[31] God and Satan are two opposite "arch-models." Many Qurʾānic verses speak of this opposition without falling into the theological dualism typical of Iranian religions:

- The ethical principle is based on the choice between the imitation of the model, *mathal*, of God, or the model of Satan. Faith in life after death is intricately linked to the divine model, representing the believer's responsibility before God for his choices and actions. It is the birth of the ethical and responsible individual, against the unconscious mass:

> Those who do not believe in the Hereafter set a bad example (*mathal*, also means "model," "similarity"), while God sets the Highest Example. He is the Mighty, the Wise. (16, 60)

- The opposition between the way of Peace, which is divine, and the steps of Satan that lead to war and violence:

> O believers! Enter the peace, all of you, and follow not the steps of Satan; he is a manifest enemy to you. (2, 208). See also (2, 168), (6, 142), (24, 21).

- The opposition between the promises of Satan and the promises of God:

> Satan promises you poverty and urges you to immorality (sin); but God promises you forgiveness from Himself, and grace. God is Embracing and Knowing. (2, 268)

- To fight for the cause of God or to fight for the cause of Satan:

> Those who believe fight in the cause of God, while those who disbelieve fight in the cause of *ṭāghūt* (evil). So, fight the allies of Satan. Surely, Satan's scheming is truly weak. (4, 76)

- Mentioning God clears the confusion caused by Satan:

> When a suggestion from Satan assails you, take refuge with God. He is Hearing and Knowing. Those who are righteous, when an impulse from Satan strikes them, they remind themselves, and immediately see clearly. (7, 200–201)

Satan and the Soul

In his explanation of the nature of the devil, Girard states that Satan "does not have a stable foundation; he has no *being* at all. To clothe himself in the semblance of being, he must act as a parasite on God's creatures. He is totally mimetic, which amounts to saying *nonexistent as an individual self*."[32] Satan is rather a mechanism; it is the logic of evil, a way of seeing and acting.

Although the Qur'ān speaks of Satan on several occasions, his absence is noted in the story of the two sons of Adam, which will be explained further.

TABLE 2. The Soul and Satan in the Qur'ān

Action	Soul	Satan
Sawwala (v.): To induce, entice, to beguile, prompt, to talk into bad ideas	And they [Joseph's brothers] brought his shirt, with fake blood on it. He [Jacob] said, "*Your souls enticed you to do something*. But patience is beautiful, and God is my Help against what you describe." (12, 18). See also (12, 83). He [the builder of the golden calf] said, "I saw what they did not see, so I grasped a handful from the Messenger's traces, and I flung it away. Thus, *my soul prompted me*." (20, 96)	Those who reverted after the guidance became clear to them, *Satan has enticed them* and has given them latitude. (47, 25)
Ammāra bi-al-sūʾ: Having the tendency of commanding evil	[Joseph:] "Yet I do not claim to be innocent. *The soul commands evil,* except those on whom my Lord has mercy." (12, 53)	*He [Satan] commands you to do evil* and vice, and to say about God what you do not know. (2, 169)

We see how the figure of Satan has been replaced by "satanic" actions such as jealousy, seduction, and, in the end, murder.

Another feature that shows Satan's invisible presence or active absence is his whisper, *waswasa*, a low and quite inaudible voice, as indicated by the word's Arabic phonics. This voice is internalized, to the point that the man thinks it is the voice of his own thought and adopts it as his own will, discovering afterward that it is nothing but alienation and perdition.

You can understand Satan's whisper as an extension of the ego, the dark side of the soul, *nafs*. Satan's hidden voice sounds in the emptiness of the soul, in its fear, despair, sadness, or on the contrary, he plays with its ambitions, greed, and illusions of grandeur. In some Qurʾānic verses, we find that the human soul can have satanic characteristics, especially in narrative scenes where Satan is absent.

The soul that induces evil, *al-nafs al-ammāra bi-al-sūʾ*, is only one dimension of the human being; it is just one possibility. The Qurʾān also speaks of other aspects and levels: the soul as critical conscience, *al-nafs al-lawwāma* (75, 2), and of the serene and pacified soul, *al-nafs al-muṭmaʾinna*, content and contented, *rāḍiya marḍiyya* (86, 27–28). They are psychic and spiritual levels in the way to God. In any case, the satanic whispering does not have a driving power over man and cannot cancel human responsibilities:

> "Surely, Satan's scheming is truly weak" (4, 76); its relative strength lies precisely in human weakness; "man has been created weak" (4, 28). This same weakness is called "the soul that commands evil" (12, 53).

> When the matter is all over [the Last Judgment], Satan will say, "God has promised you the promise of truth, and I promised you, but I failed you. I had no authority over you, except that I called you, and you answered me. So do not blame me but blame yourselves. I cannot come to your aid, nor can you come to my aid. I reject your associating with me in the past." (14, 22)

> Like Satan when he tells man to disbelieve, but when he disbelieves, he says, "I am absolved of you. Indeed, I fear God, the Lord of all the worlds." (59, 16)

Satan's declaration of innocence, his handwashing, is correct. In the end, the responsibility is individual, and no one decides in the place of the other person or forces him or her to do what he or she does not want to do. The same declaration of innocence is attributed to men in their conflicts and failed alliances:

> [In the Last Judgment], those who were followed will then disown those who followed them, and they will see the retribution, and ties between them will be severed. Those who followed will say, "If only we can have another chance, we will disown them, as they disowned us." Thus, God will show them their deeds, as regrets to them, and they will not come out of the Fire. (2, 166–167)

Satan, as René Girard explains, is "a kind of personification of 'bad contagion,' just as much in its conflictive and disintegrative aspects as in its reconciling and unifying aspects . . . [he] is the one who foments disorder, the one who sows scandals, and then at the height of the crises that he himself provokes, Satan suddenly brings them to an end by expelling the disorder. Satan expels Satan by means of innocent victims whom he succeeds in having condemned."[33] In his provocation, as well as in his self-expulsion, he seems absent and invisible. The peace of Satan is false; it is only a truce between two wars, an ephemeral satisfaction that is replaced by bitterness and regret, as the preceding verses indicate.

Satan and Power

The Antichrist

Satan's active absence occurs in satanic human figures in the Qur'ān and the prophetic Tradition, such as the figure of the Antichrist, found only in the Sunna. He is called al-Masīḥ al-Dajjāl, the imposter (deceiver) Christ, or simply Dajjāl, or sometimes Masīkh, which is a play on words by replacing the letter *ḥ* of Masīḥ with *kh*, so the meaning becomes "disfigured," or "deformed." Let us take a look at these sayings attributed to the Prophet Muḥammad:

> Dajjāl will appear with water and fire. What the people will assume to be water will actually be fire that burns, and what they assume to be fire will actually be cool, sweet water. Any of you who meet him should jump into what appears as fire because it is actually pure, sweet water.

In another ḥadīth:

> He is one-eyed and will bring with him something like Paradise and Hell; but what he calls Paradise will be in fact Hell. . . . Every Prophet warned his community about the one-eyed liar. He is one-eyed and your Lord (God) is not one-eyed. Written between his eyes are [the letters] *kāf*, *fā*, *rā* (that is *kāfir*, unbeliever).[34]

In this tyrannical figure, we find several satanic characteristics, including the scandal of lies, calling water fire, and Heaven Hell. It is unbelief that speaks in God's name, indeed makes himself God with a false power to send people to Heaven or Hell. This story is in harmony with what Girard says: Satan imitates God "in a manner that is jealous, grotesque, perverse, and as contrary as possible to the upright and obedient imitation of Jesus

. . . [Satan's] kingdom is a caricature of the kingdom of God. Satan is the ape of God."[35] In the same way, false Christians, like the Antichrist, pretend to imitate Jesus but are devoured by mimetic rivalries and superficial imitation.[36] The same observation is valid for Muslims who seem extremely attached to religion in form and appearance, but in reality betray the spirit and meaning, as described in this ḥadīth:

> There shall emerge from among you a group of people who will cause you to consider your own prayers deficient when compared to theirs, or your own fasting deficient when compared to theirs, or your own deeds deficient when compared to theirs. They will recite the Qurʾān, but it does not go beyond their throats. They exit from Islam just like an arrow passes through the body of the hunter's prey: the hunter looks at the arrowhead and sees no evidence that it penetrated the prey; the hunter looks at the shaft and sees no evidence that it penetrated the prey; the hunter looks at the fletching and sees no evidence that it penetrated the prey; and he looks at the notch at the arrow's end skeptically, to see whether it has any traces of blood from the prey.[37]

Pharaoh and His Entourage

In the Prophets' Qurʾānic stories, the unconscious crowd is manipulated by a conscious mind, which directs the crowd behind the scenes to serve the interests of the dominant group. The stories of the Prophets reveal this mechanism of abuse and manipulation; however, the same stories illustrate that the good always exists and that the free and critical human conscience never fails, even when it is hugely outnumbered or represented by only one person. For this reason, the Prophets risk every time becoming a scapegoat and perfect victim, which threatens the social (unjust) order and which must be sacrificed to find (illusionary) peace. This opposition between the Prophets, who represent the voice of God and critical conscience, on the one hand, and the crowd, and behind it *al-malaʾ*, the power elite, is a main feature of this literary genre. The Prophets are persecuted not only by the crowd but also by the entourage of the Pharaoh, *al-malaʾ*, by the powerful and manipulative leadership, also called in the Qurʾān: *mustakbirūn*, the arrogant people, which is a satanic adjective par excellence. Again, Satan seems absent, but his divisive logic is more active than ever through satanic human figures.

The pharaonic power despises the crowd and believes that it is incapable of thinking and deciding and that its salvation is in following this power blindly:

> Pharaoh said, "I do not show you except what I see, and I do not guide you except to the path of rectitude." (40, 29)

> Thus, he fooled (despised, treated lightly) his people, and they obeyed him. They were wicked people. (43, 54)

From this perspective, we understand the opposition of Moses, revealing the hypocrisy of the Pharaoh, who does not call oppression by his real name. Instead, he considers it as favor and charity:

> [Moses replied:] This is the favor with which you taunt me that you have enslaved the Children of Israel? (26, 22)

In conclusion, in the Qurʾān, there are three levels of satanic presence:

1. An explicit presence, where Satan is mentioned by name: as, for example, in the story of the creation of Adam and Eve, the sin and the Fall.
2. An implicit presence, where the name of Satan is absent, but very present through his seduction and violence mechanisms, as in the story of the two sons of Adam.
3. In other stories, in a more complex social dynamism, Satan is represented by the symbols of power who know how to use satanic manipulation. The most eloquent example is Pharaoh and his entourage. The Prophets, on the other hand, are always in conflict with this ruling class. The corrupt consciences of the leaders manipulate the unconscious crowd to shut out the Prophets' critical voice.

In the Gospel, Jesus's Passion clearly shows the mechanism of satanic manipulation, led by religious and political leaders. Regardless of the victims' final fate, the satanic logic, as described in the Qurʾānic stories, is the same systematic and organized violence suffered by Jesus. Girard quotes Peter: "The kings of the earth took their stand and the rulers were gathered together against the Lord and his anointed."[38] Peter refers to a special relationship between the Cross and power, which is rooted in collective murders analogous to that of Jesus. Without being the same as Satan, the powers are all tributaries of him. They are all tributaries of the false divinities generated by Satan. He is the lying religious who protects men from violence and chaos through sacrificial rites. This system is rooted in illusion, but its action in the world is real, to the extent that false transcendences can make themselves obeyed.[39]

Thirst for Peace

"To escape from animal instinct and arrive at mimetic desire with all its dangers of mimetic conflicts, humans have to discipline their desire, and they cannot accomplish that except by means of sacrifices. Humanity springs forth from religion, i.e., from many 'founding murders' and the rituals that spring from them."[40] It is evident here that Girard gives to religion, even the satanic and sacrificial one, a role of pacification, which remains provisional.

The human thirst for Peace goes beyond this temporary truce, and this illusory pause. For this reason, the Hebrew Shalōm and Arabic *al-Salām* cannot be translated simply with superficial peace. Instead, they indicate permanent and profound Peace, a divine and inclusive one:

- *Al-Salām*, the Peace, is one of the beautiful divine Names in the Qur'ān, which should be reflected in the life of believers:

> He is God. There is no god but He, the Knower of secrets and declarations. He is the Compassionate, the Merciful. He is God; besides Whom there is no god; the Sovereign, the Holy, the Peace (*al-Salām*), the Faith-Giver, the Overseer, the Almighty, the Omnipotent, the Overwhelming. Glory be to God, beyond what they associate. He is God; the Creator, the Maker, the Designer. His are the most beautiful Names. Whatever is in the heavens and the earth glorifies Him. He is the Majestic, the Wise. (59, 22–24)

- The divine message transmitted by all the Prophets throughout history is a message that invites to the ways of Peace to the point of dwelling in Peace; "the Abode of Peace" is one of Paradise's names in the Qur'ān, in this world and in the other:

> God guides with it [the Book] whoever follows His approval to *the ways of Peace*, and He brings them out of darkness into light, by His permission, and He guides them in a straight path. (5, 16 the emphasis is mine)

> God invites to *the Abode of Peace*, and guides whomever He wills to a straight path. (10, 25 the emphasis is mine). See also (6, 127).

> Therein [in Heaven] they will hear no vain talk or sinful speech, but only the greeting: "Peace, Peace." (56, 25–26). See also (25, 75).

- Peace, which is God Himself and willed by Him, is not only an eschatological promise but accompanies the believer in all stages of life and beyond, as Jesus Christ says in the Qur'ān:

> Peace on me the day I was born, and the day I die, and the day I am raised alive. (19, 33). See also (19, 15) about John the Baptist.

Peace is linked to another divine Name and central Qur'ānic value: Mercy, *Raḥma*. The only divine Name to have the same value as the proper Name *Allāh*, God, is *al-Raḥmān*, which means fullness of Mercy and Love. It coincides with another Name with the same root, *al-Raḥīm*, the Clement, the Merciful. Both derive from *r.ḥ.m.*, from which also derives *raḥim*, maternal uterus. The *basmala*, or the Qur'ānic formula *b-ism Allāh al-Raḥmān al-Raḥīm*, often translated as in the Name of God the Clement and the Merciful, is repeated 114 times in the Qur'ān.[41] *Raḥma* is divine Love concretely expressed; humans have this ability to distinguish between feeling and action, but for God, the Word is creation: to love is to give, nurture, create, and recreate. For God, the One, there is no separation between ideal and real. Therefore, Mercy is Love realized and fulfilled in creation.[42] Mercy is not only the Truth of the divine Being but also His absolute commitment, as this verse indicates:

> He has inscribed for Himself Mercy. (6, 12)

It is the only time in which we find this expression in the Qur'ān, as the only divine commitment. That means that the truth and the end of every creation are Mercy. Consequently, the only *raison d'être* of Muḥammad's mission is to bring divine Mercy everywhere, to the whole world, even more to all worlds, because true love is universal and expansive, without limits or borders:

> [O Muḥammad] We did not send you except as Mercy towards all the worlds. (21, 107)

Alongside Mercy, the Prophets' mission has as its central and permanent content: the invitation to recognize the One God and to adore Him:

> We never sent a Messenger before you without inspiring him that: "There is no god but I, so worship Me." (21, 25)

The Image of God in the Qur'ān cannot be complete without this fundamental Name: The One, *al-Aḥad*, which represents the thread that unites all the Names. It is the Name from which the belief in God's Oneness, *tawḥīd*, is derived, which has a significant impact on mimetic desire.

As a monotheistic religion, Islam emphasizes the importance of having God as the only and last "desire." The unification of desires is liberation from all desires, just as the adoration of the One God is liberation from any attachment and idol. On several occasions, the Qur'ān insists on the need to direct desire toward God, as the only finality and satisfaction of human desire. The uniqueness of God is translated into the uniqueness of desire and love, *raghba*:

> Unto God we are full of desire (or we turn our desires to Him). (9, 59). See also (68, 32).

> When you have finished, get up and turn your desire to your Lord. (94, 7–8)

Polytheism, or rather associationism, *shirk*, in Qur'ānic terminology, is seen as fragmentation and dispersion of desires, leading to a shattered soul and a slow and tormented death. One dies with every desire that escapes or vanishes.

The alternative to God is the idol, which is, par excellence, the ego. In the previous verses, desire is expressed with the verb *raghiba*, which means desire or aspire, neutrally for better or for worse. In this case, it is positive because it is oriented toward God, the absolute Good. On the other hand, when the desire is negative and selfish, it is called *hawā*, passion, which is from the same root as *hawā*ʾ, which means air or wind. Evil and selfish desire is like the air: light, dispersive, unstable, totally taken by emotions, and continually changing direction. When the ego's vain desire is blindly obeyed, it becomes a self-worshipped idol:

> Have you seen him who chose his desire as his god? (25, 43). See also (45, 23).

Malefic desire is called also *hasad*, envy or jealousy:

> Do they envy the people for what God has given them of His grace? (4, 54). The same word is used in different contexts: (2, 109), (48, 15), (113, 5).

We also find the term *shahwa*, desire, often in the negative sense:

> Adorned for the people is the love of desires, such as women, and children, and piles upon piles of gold and silver, and branded horses, and livestock, and fields. These are the conveniences of the worldly life, but with God lies the finest resort. (3, 14)

> God intends to redeem you, but those who follow their desires want you to turn away utterly. (4, 27). See also (7, 81), (16, 57), (19, 59), (27, 55), (34, 54).

The ego gives as a false feeling of autonomy and independence, like small divinities on earth, as the Qurʾān says:

> Yet man behaves arrogantly, because he thinks himself self-sufficient. (96, 6–7)

Girard explains well this arrogant self-sufficiency: "Often we believe we are imitating the true God, but we are really imitating only false models of the independent self that cannot be wounded or defeated."[43] The small, inflated egos are usually associated with the pharaonic egos of power, "we feel that we are at the point of attaining autonomy as we imitate our models of power and prestige. This autonomy, however, is really nothing but a reflection of the illusions projected by our admiration for them."[44] Only God is the Self-sufficient, *al-Ghanī*; humans are needy and poor, and their salvation is properly in the awareness of their ontological poverty and thirst for God:

> O mankind! It is you who stand in need of God, God is Self-sufficient, and Praiseworthy. (35, 15). See also (47, 38).

The transformative and educational mission of religion is to purify and unify the soul and desire:

> Successful is he who purifies it [the soul]. Failing is he who corrupts it. (91, 8–9). See also (87, 14). It is a question of a spiritual success, *falāḥ*.

All Islamic rituals are aimed at educating the soul, purifying from the prohibited desires, and unifying it:

> The prayer prevents indecencies and evils. And the remembrance of God is greater. (29, 45)

Patience, *ṣabr*, the control of emotions and desires, especially anger, is a supreme value repeatedly recommended in the Qur'ān and in the prophetic Tradition, which includes several other values such as forgiveness:

> So be patient, with beautiful patience. (70, 5)

> O you who believe! Seek help through patience and prayers. God is with the patient. (2, 153). See also (2, 249), (8, 46, 66).

> Those who avoid major sins and indecencies; and if they become angry, they forgive. (42, 37)

> Those who give in prosperity and adversity, and those who restrain anger, and those who forgive people. God loves the doers of good. (3, 134)

To reach a high level of self-control, we need a critical conscience that refuses to follow blindly in the ancestors' footsteps and questions the parents' inheritance. Before the ancestral traditions, there was the prophetic rebellion:

> When it is said to them, "Come to what God has revealed, and to the Messenger," they say, "Sufficient for us is what we found our forefathers upon." Even if their forefathers knew nothing, and were not guided? (5, 104)

It is the same conscience that always asks:

> Produce your proof, if you are truthful (2, 111). See also (27, 64).

A conscience that does not accept any news without verifying its authenticity:

> O you who believe! If a troublemaker brings you any news, investigate, lest you harm people out of ignorance, and you become regretful for what you have done. (49, 6)

These principles and values are valid even today against any fundamentalism or populism. Here, we are faced with different religiosity types, which are found within the same faith, and within the heart of every man. A person, with these ethical qualities and values, is difficult to manipulate by the crowd and those who hold the ranks behind the scenes. It is the birth of the individual, which is not a modern invention. The Qur'ān repeatedly emphasizes that responsibility is individual and personal:

> No burden-bearer shall bear another's burden, and if some over-laden soul should call out for someone else to carry his load, not the least portion of it will be borne for him, even though he were a near relative. (35, 18). See also (6, 164), (17, 15), (39, 7).

Sufism, Islamic spirituality, has developed the central doctrine of Islam, the Oneness of God, *tawḥīd*, in an ethical and practical way: believing in the One God means the unification and integration of the soul, dedicating the whole life to God, as reflected in the Qur'ānic prayer:

> Say, "My prayer and my worship, and my life and my death, are devoted to God, the Lord of the worlds." (6, 162)

Recognizing God's Oneness means getting out of the state of dispersion and fragmentation, to unite the soul and desire and orient them toward the One God, harmonizing the soul after being divided between different desires. This soul, united in desire and will, succeeds in seeing God everywhere, succeeds in intuiting the One's Presence in the creation. Rūmī (m. 672/1273) describes this concept perfectly:

> I once had twenty thousand desires. In my passion for Him, no desire remained.[45]

In his poem *The Theophany of Perfection*, Ibn ʿArabī (638/1240) describes the other side, God's Desire of being desired, which is the deep meaning of the verse "I did not create the jinn and the humans except to worship Me" (51, 56).[46] God speaks in the first person:

> Oh, my beloved! How many times I have called you without your hearing Me!
> How many times I have shown myself without your looking at Me!
> How many times I have become perfume without your inhaling Me!
> How many times I have become food without your tasting Me!
> How is it that you do not smell Me in what you breathe?
> How do you not see Me, not hear Me?
> I am more delicious than anything delicious,
> *More desirable than anything desirable,*
> More perfect than anything perfect.
> I am Beauty and Grace!
> Love Me and love nothing else
> *Desire Me*
> *Let Me be your sole concern to the exclusion of all concerns!*
> (the emphasis is mine)[47]

Pluralism as a Divine Will

Among the techniques used by the Qur'ān to free the human being from the negative desire that leads to rivalry and division, is to transform the desire into an engine of positive competition. The same energy, which can be oriented toward destruction and violence, becomes constructive and peaceful, when it is oriented toward the common good, unity and service. The desire that can manifest itself in "pious" jealousy, leading to religious exclusivism and violence in God's name, becomes a "race for good." In this way, rivalitarian mimetism is transformed into salvific mimetism; whoever claims to be on the right path must show how far he or she can achieve excellence because of his or her faith. Orthopraxis becomes a criterion of orthodoxy:

> To every community is a direction towards which it turns. Therefore, race towards goodness. Wherever you may be, God will bring you all together. (2, 148)

> For each of you We have assigned a law and a method. Had God willed, He could have made you a single community, but He tests you through what He has given you. So, race towards goodness. To God is your return, all of you; then He will inform you of what you had disputed. (5, 48)

> And do not be like her who unravels her yarn, breaking it into pieces, after she has spun it strongly. Nor use your oaths[48] as means of deception among you, because one community is more prosperous than another. God is testing you thereby. On the Day of Resurrection, He will make clear to you everything you had disputed about. Had God willed, He would have made you one community, but He leaves astray whom He wills, and He guides whom He wills. And you will surely be questioned about what you used to do. And do not use your oaths to deceive one another, so that a foot may not slip after being firm, and you taste misery because you hindered from God's path and incur a terrible torment. And do not exchange God's covenant for a small price. What is with God is better for you if you only knew. What you have runs out, but what is with God remains. We will reward those who are patient according to the best of their deeds. Whoever works righteousness, whether male or female, while being a believer, We will grant him a good life, and We will reward them according to the best of what they used to do. (16, 92–97)

"Rivalistic desires are all the more overwhelming since they reinforce one another,"[49] as Girard confirms. So do religious exclusivisms; they confirm each other, united in division and hatred. Exclusivism is potential violence, which increases among similar protagonists: the more they resemble each other, the more they hate each other. The following verses explain well the mechanism of exclusivism, which arises from the closest religions and despite the common background that unites them, as in the case of the Abrahamic religions:

> In fact, whoever submits himself to God, and is a doer of good, will have his reward with his Lord, they have nothing to fear, nor shall they grieve. The Jews say, "The Christians are not based on anything"; and the Christians say, "The Jews are not based on anything." Yet they both read the Scripture. Similarly, the ignorant said the same thing. God will judge between them on the Day of Resurrection regarding their differences. Who is more unjust than him who forbids the remembrance of God's name in places of worship, and contributes to their ruin? These ought not to enter them except in fear. For them is disgrace in this world, and for them is a terrible punishment in the Hereafter. (2, 112–114)

Exclusivism generates a type of religiosity, which can demand obedience to God but hides idolatry, absolutizing the collective ego, the great We, the community as a tribe. As Girard says: "The idolatry is necessarily associated with the idolization of ourselves."[50]

Paradoxically, Girard does not look positively at the theology of religious pluralism. He believes in Christian "singularity," if not to say "superiority." Christianity not only denounces the collective violence and announces the innocence of the victim, as happens in the Hebrew Bible and the Qurʾān, but also announces the divinity of the Victim, par excellence, Jesus Christ, what the other Abrahamic religions do not. The significant similarity with myth makes Christianity, according to Girard, more radical in its opposition and ability to demythologize it. This same similarity could be seen by an outsider as a "compromise" or an identification with the mythical religions.

Girard considers that the theology of religious pluralism fails to appreciate Christian "uniqueness," risking relativism: "Christianity has been losing ground for centuries in the Western world, a decline that continues to accelerate. Now not only isolated individuals abandon the churches, but entire churches, led by their clergy, switch their allegiance and go over to the camp of 'pluralism.' This pluralism is relativism that claims it is 'more Christian' than the adherence to dogma because it is 'kinder' and more 'tolerant' toward non-Christian religions."[51] Girard fails to see in pluralism a possibility to dissolve violent mimetism, creating, as the Qur'ān says, good mimetism as a competition for good, without necessarily falling into relativism. Unfortunately, Girard's description of theological pluralism is somewhat caricatural.

The Meaning of the Cross

The Cross is central in Girard's thought, because it disproves all mythology, declaring the victim's innocence. "The Cross and the mechanism of Satan are one," as Jesus "says just before his arrest: 'This is your hour, and the power of darkness.'"[52] The Qur'ān, on the other hand, seems to deny the Crucifixion, and this denial has marked Islamic thought throughout history. Faced with this seemingly insurmountable obstacle, how can we understand, if not appreciate, the Cross and its salvific meaning in the face of violence?

A careful study of the history of Islamic thought shows that there is no consensus on denying the Crucifixion,[53] which nevertheless remains the dominant position to this day. The verse that would justify the denial is the following:

> And for their saying, "We have killed the Christ, Jesus, the son of Mary, the Messenger of God." In fact, they did not kill him, nor did they crucify him, but *shubbiha* (it appeared) to them. Indeed, those who differ about him are in doubt about it. They have no knowledge of it, except the following of assumptions. Certainly, they did not kill him. Rather, God raised him up to Himself. God is Mighty and Wise. (4, 157–158)

The verse reads: "They did not kill him, nor did they crucify him, but *shubbiha* to them." This ambiguous verb, *shubbiha*, was at the center of the hermeneutical debate:

- *Shubbiha*, which is the passive form of the verb *shabbaha*, could be derived from *shabah*, resemblance, from which the translation seemed, appeared. This understanding permitted the legend of the substitution, which pretends that another man was crucified instead of Jesus.[54]
- It could also be derived from *shubha*, which means confusion,

> ambiguity, uncertainty. In this way, the verse can be translated as: "they have been led into confusion." The Crucifixion is seen here as a state of confusion, a scandal, *fitna*: Apparently, everything was in order on the religious level, as on the political level; after two solemn courts, the execution was formally "legal," but in truth, it was a crime, the killing of an innocent victim. This false victory is exposed carefully by the Qur'ān: they have not won at all; they failed ethically and in God's eyes. The sacrificial religion uses the law to betray the spirit, practicing formal and violent justice. It is not a judgment against a specific religious group, but rather a trans-religious phenomenon, a blasphemy in God's name, an anti-religious religion, and a homicidal theology. The *tashbīh* is the inability to distinguish between good and evil, or the ability to confuse people, to manipulate and deceive them. In this confusion, everything looks like everything, and everything is the same; there is no more choice, and therefore there is no more ethics.

Muslims who do not see in verse (4, 157) a denial of the Crucifixion, interpret it metaphorically, in light of other verses that confirm the triumph of the divine Word:[55]

> They want to extinguish God's Light with their mouths, but God refuses except to complete His Light, even though the disbelievers dislike it. (9, 32)

> [God] made the word of those who disbelieved the lowest, while the Word of God is the Highest. God is Mighty and Wise. (9, 40)

Consider also that the Qur'ān exalts martyrdom (3, 169) and recognizes the martyrdom of the Prophets (3, 181), (4, 155), which does not contradict any Islamic doctrine.

On the spiritual level, what matters is not the Cross itself, but the transformative alchemy that allows the conversion within every human being, the death and resurrection of each one. The Cross is genuinely able to eradicate violence from the heart, as Girard affirms, only when it becomes an inner experience.

The Cross represents a "real symbol" that allows conversion to God, the essential transformation without which religion has no meaning. This fundamental spiritual experience is not often expressed in Christological terms for Muslims, as in the ḥadīth attributed to the Prophet Muḥammad: "Die before you die,"[56] similar to the Franciscan prayer: "It is in dying that one is raised to eternal life."[57] Conversion is the death of the ego and the rediscovery or emergence of the true Self, the divine Spirit into the human being. It is the actualization of potential sainthood, which is the purpose of creation. It is the inner meaning of *shahāda*, the Islamic testimony of faith:

> *Lā ilāh*[a] *illā Allāh*, no god but God, negation + affirmation
>
> *Lā ilāh*[a], no god (*fanā'*, annihilation) = Death of ego, false divinities, and perverted desires in the heart
>
> *illā Allāh*, but God (*baqā'*, permanence) = resurrection, manifestation of the real Self

The same meaning is expressed in the Sufi interpretation of the story of the golden calf in the Qur'ān:

> And recall that Moses said to his people, "O my people, you have done wrong to yourselves by worshiping the calf. So repent to your Maker, and kill your egos." (2, 54)

Al-Sulamī (d. 412/1021) commented: "the calf of every human being is his ego." Then added: "The first step in servanthood, *'ubūdiyya*, is repentance, which is: destroying and killing the ego, *nafs*, abandoning desires and cutting off [one's self] from the ambition."[58]

For Christians, the death and Resurrection of Jesus is the "means" that leads to the same thing that Muslims seek, but with a different language and through other symbols. It is possible to appreciate the essential, regardless of the form and expression. The Qur'ān speaks in a practical way of the need to overcome the ego by serving others. It is the difficult ascending path that each of us must take:

> But he did not brave the ascent. And what will explain to you what the ascent is? The freeing of a slave. Or the feeding on a day of hunger. An

> orphan near of kin. Or a destitute in the dust. Then he becomes of those who believe, and advise one another to patience, and advise one another to kindness. These are the people of happiness. (90, 11–18)

The death and Resurrection of Jesus Christ find their full meaning in light of his life. A life of truth and sincerity, a dangerous and demanding life. His death on the Cross is the consequence of his testimony. Martyrdom is testimony in life before death. The Resurrection is the triumph of the fundamental values that are immortal, the blood that conquers the sword, where death does not have the last word! Paul expresses this triumph of the Cross in this way:

> [Christ has] canceled the accusation that stands against us with its legal claims. He set it aside, nailing it to the cross. He thus disarmed the principalities and powers and made a public spectacle of them, drawing them along in his triumph.[59]

In Jesus's words and behavior, we find profound critiques of formalism, ritualism, legalism, and all the evils that stiffen the religious soul, transforming it from a force of peace into an instrument of domination and exclusion. The life and discourse of Jesus are against the subtle and hidden idolatry of arrogant religious people, often violent or allies of violent political leaders. This prophetic discourse, very present in the Qurʾān, unmasks Satan's lies and declares the innocence of the victims.

According to René Girard, Jesus Christ represents a decisive model in breaking the mimetic chain of violence, which has marked the mythology of ancient religions. The art of breaking with violence, which Jesus teaches, is vital: how not to fall into the logic of evil, into the trap of violent mimetism. He is a significant model for those who believe in nonviolent resistance. Islamic theology of nonviolence cannot ignore Jesus as a source of inspiration. Even Muslim liberation theologians, like their Christian precursors, find in the rebellious life of Jesus an inspiration for a high sense of justice, solidarity with the oppressed, the weak, and the marginalized. It is an example of how to lead an ascetic life dedicated to simple people and those far from the palaces of power, a free life, which resists the temptation of power, money, and hypocrisy.[60]

It is possible to read "Jesus forsaken on the Cross" symbolically in harmony with the Islamic faith, seeing in this Christian doctrine the deeper meaning of *islām*, as a radical submission to the divine Will and as a total liberation of the ego. It is the meaning of *tawakkul*, surrender entirely to God, or *riḍā*, spiritual satisfaction, which Christian de Chergé (d. 1996) mentioned in a Christmas homily (1994), explaining the meaning of "Jesus forsaken."[61]

"The resurrection of Christ owes nothing to the human violence,"[62] as Girard affirms, because "the Word of God is the Highest" (9, 40). The Cross is nothing but the prostration, *sujūd*, of the servant, risen and elevated into God. It is the majesty of humility when nothingness becomes the Whole. Only in this way, violence is defeated, and Satan is stoned. The Resurrection is not the fruit of violence but its antidote. Violence does not win against the victim; it is the victim who wins. The victim does not die, because the human being in truth is eternal; he or she does nothing but reveal God, remove evil's masks and arrogant claims, and make God nearer and more visible.

The Divine Models

All these values and educational methods, mentioned above directly and conceptually, are embodied in the Prophets, in a narrative way throughout the Qur'ān, the Tradition of Prophet Muḥammad, the Sunna, and in his biography, the Sīra, all of which represent a model of ethical excellence for Muslims. "The tenth commandment signals a revolution and prepares the way for it. This revolution comes to fruition in the New Testament,"[63] as Girard affirms, and it continues to flourish in the Islamic sources, as a Muslim would say.

Girard defines the divine model in this manner: "[Jesus] asks us to imitate him; it is to turn us away from mimetic rivalries." Indeed, he "invites us to imitate his own *desire*, the spirit that directs him toward the goal on which his intention is fixed: to resemble God the Father as much as possible . . . His goal is to become the perfect *image* of God . . . He invites us to imitate his own imitation . . . neither the Father nor the Son desires greedily, egotistically." "If we imitate the detached generosity of God, then the trap of mimetic rivalries will never close over us. This is why Jesus says also, 'Ask, and it will be given to you'"[64] (Mt 7, 7), and as the Qur᾿ān says: "Your Lord said: call me and I will answer you" (40, 60).

The detached generosity and love are manifested in the prophetic mission, summarized in this Qur᾿ānic formula, repeatedly mentioned by the Prophets:

> Say: I do not ask of you any reward other than love of neighbor. (42, 23). See also (6, 90), (26, 109, 127, 145, 164, 180), (11, 29, 51), (25, 57), (38, 86).

The sense of imitation explained by Girard, concerning Jesus, represents an excellent explanation of the profound meaning of the concept of the Sunna in Islam, as an imitation of the soul of the Prophet, described in the Qur᾿ān as *ʿuswa ḥasana*, a good and beautiful example (33, 21). The same title is used for Abraham (60, 4, 6), and valid for all the Prophets. The imitation of the Prophet is nothing more than embracing the divine Will, getting out of our ego, and being free. Imitating a person free from ego means imitating God and staying in God. The will of the Prophet can be imitated because it is God's Will:

> Your friend [Muḥammad] has not gone astray, nor has he erred. Nor does he speak out of desire (*hawā*). It is but a revelation revealed. Taught to him by the Extremely Powerful. (53, 3–5)

> Say, obey God and the Messenger. (3, 32, 132). See also (4, 59), (5, 92), (8, 1, 20, 46), (24, 54), (47, 33), (58, 13), (64, 12).

Girard points out that "Jesus never scorns the Law, even when it takes the form of prohibitions. . . . The disadvantage of the prohibitions, however, is that they do not finally play their role in a satisfying manner. Their primarily negative character, as St. Paul well understood, inevitably provokes in us the mimetic urge to transgress them. The best way to preventing violence does not consist in forbidding objects, or even Rivalistic desire, as the tenth commandment does, but in offering to people the model that will protect them from mimetic rivalries."[65] For this reason, the formalistic and legalistic religiosity, based solely on prohibitions, fails ethically.

The law is not enough without an inner transformation and a reorientation of desire, with the help of a living master, as a divine model, who is the continuity of arch-models like Jesus and Muḥammad. The model shows that the liberation from mimetic rivalries is possible and not only a mere idea. If it was possible once, that means it is possible twice. The master becomes a mirror, in which we see ourselves in order to transform the selfish desire, *hawā*, to a divine desire, *islām*, a convinced voluntary submission to God. Therefore, the Sunna, when it is limited to imitating the Prophet in doing, without imitating him in the soul and inner life, risks being counterproductive. The model, *ʿuswa*, must be good and beautiful, *hasana*, inspired by the Prophet's purified heart.

The models of sainthood and prophecy show that "mimetic desire is intrinsically good," and "without mimetic desire there would be neither freedom nor humanity."[66] All education is based on mimetism, in different forms, called either Sunna or Tradition.

The "conscious" mimetism of human models of sainthood is against any "unconscious" mimetism, based on manipulation, domination, tribalism, nationalism, or religious exclusivism. For that reason, the Qurʾān warns us not to uncritically follow the ancestors or the leaders.

Practical Ethics

In this last part of the chapter, we identify a series of ethical principles and practices that aim to reduce or eliminate violence:

No Compulsion in Religion

We do not find the word "nonviolence" in the Qurʾān. Instead, we see the expression "no compulsion" in the verse:

> *There is no compulsion in religion*; *rushd* (good sense, good judgment, correctness, rectitude, wisdom, maturity) stands out clear from *ghayy* (misguidedness, delusion, error): whoever rejects evil and believes in God has grasped the most trustworthy hand-hold, that never breaks. And God hears and knows all things. (2, 256, the emphasis is mine)

"Non-compulsion" is stronger and more radical than "nonviolence" because it rejects even psychological violence, a hidden form without shedding blood or leaving bruises, but leads to physical violence by preparing its conditions. The verse "No Compulsion in Religion" is not only a fundamental moral principle, but is also, in itself, a definition of religion. Religion does not combine with coercion, which ranges between violence by hand and weapons and violence with words and gestures, and extends to silence and neglect. Non-compulsion is a categorical rejection of all forms of violence: what is visible and invisible, by brutality or by temptation, seduction, and the exploitation of weaknesses and needs. Non-compulsion is a purification of religion from all impurities that would doubt or diminish human free choice. Embracing or leaving a religion,[67] practicing or abandoning it are all possible options for a person as long as he or she is free and responsible. Anyone who thinks that an external authority (state or law) can make a good believer is wrong. Coercion only makes hypocrites or fearful, oppressed people. Coercion is a psychological terror that enslaves and does not liberate, is anti-religious, and is contrary to the essence of belief.

The same verse continues, stating the reasons for non-compulsion: "*rushd* (truth, rectitude, wisdom, maturity) stands out clear from *ghayy* (error, ignorance)." This clear distinction can be understood on two levels: the verse affirms the dynamism and autonomy of truth on the intellectual level. It has beauty, authority, and the ability to move and persuade, which makes it distinguished from delusion and lie. It does not need violence even when it is subtle and hidden. The truth shines like a light in darkness. It does not require a protector or guardian. It crosses peoples and cultures, strong in itself and not because of others, giving goodness, beauty, and freedom. It uses people, and people do not use it. As for the practical level: coercion is oppression and injustice, which are incompatible with reason and wisdom. Coercion is satanic!

Non-compulsive religion is nonviolent par excellence:

> Those who respond to their Lord, and pray regularly, and *conduct their affairs by mutual consultation*, and give of what We have provided them. (42, 38, the emphasis is mine)

> It is by of Mercy from God that you [Muḥammad] were gentle with them. Had you been harsh, hardhearted, they would have dispersed from around you. So pardon them, and ask forgiveness for them, and *consult them in the*

> *conduct of affairs.* And when you make a decision, put your trust in God; God loves the trusting. (3, 159, the emphasis is mine)

The believers manage their affairs through consultation, *shūrā*: from the family to the state; as they pray, they consult each other. Consultation is their basic social ethics. Peace with God descends on earth as peace among people. The consultation is the first social expression of nonviolence and non-compulsion. Without consultation, tyranny and hypocrisy prevail, as two sides of the same coin.

The Syrian theologian Jawdat Said believes that Muslims have understood from the verse "There is no compulsion in religion," that if non-compulsion is a norm in religion, then it should not be compulsion *a priori* below it, and that includes "no compulsion in politics."

> For this reason, they called the Caliphs who came to power without coercion and with the approval of the Muslims: *al-Rāshidūn* (people of *rushd*, well-guided or wisemen). They did not use this title for any ruler who got power by force.[68]

The centrality of non-compulsion makes democracy—the contemporary political expression of *shūrā*—a necessary condition for achieving an atmosphere of freedom and justice that allows people to choose. Freedom of conscience and belief is an integral part of the concept of democracy and nonviolence.

Responding to Verbal Violence

The best response to violence is nonviolence, beginning by not contributing to any escalation and not creating an atmosphere of hatred that could incite physical or verbal violence. The Muslim does not offend any religion or faith, even when he does not share its doctrinal contents. The Qur'ān asks the Prophet and his Companions not to insult the divinities of others. These are precisely the idols of the Arab pagans, their most ferocious persecutors, in order not to provoke an adverse reaction and other insults against Muslims. Furthermore, because insulting is not a moral attitude:

> Do not insult those they call upon besides God, lest they insult God out of hostility and ignorance. (6, 108)

The true Muslim avoids anger, the main cause of insults and offensive words, as these ḥadīths indicate:

> A man said to the Prophet, "Advise me." The Prophet said: "Do not get angry." He repeated that several times.[69]

> Strong is not he who overcomes [his adversary] by throwing him down, but he who can control himself when angry.[70]

> The Prophet said: "One who believes in God and the Last Day must speak good or remain silent."[71]

The believer is recommended to avoid quarrels and polemics, which are often an expression of egoism and arrogance and not a way for the truth:

> The Prophet said: I guarantee a house in the surroundings of Paradise for a man who avoids quarrelling even if he were in the right, a house in the middle of Paradise for a man who avoids lying even if he were joking, and a house in the upper part of Paradise for a man who made his character good.[72]

There is no justification for responding to the offense with violence. A series of verses indicate the right answer to the provocation: ignoring it. Silence, and not anger, is the answer that extinguishes the fire of hatred and contempt. Responding to provocation with anger is to do what the provocateurs want: to ridicule the other. Silence allows one to leave the irrational emotional state and return to the normal state, the serene and rational one:

> The servants of the Merciful are those who walk the earth in humility, and when the ignorant address them, they say, "Peace." (25, 63)

> Keep to forgiveness [O Muḥammad], and enjoin kindness, and turn away from the ignorant. (7, 199)

This separation is only temporary, an opportunity to calm souls, a pause for reflection, which ends as soon as they change discourse:

> He has revealed to you in the Book that when you hear God's signs being rejected, or ridiculed, do not sit with them until they engage in some other subject. Otherwise, you would be like them. God will gather the hypocrites and the disbelievers, into Hell, altogether. (4, 140). See also (6, 68).

We see from the previous verses and many others that there is no earthly punishment for blasphemy or apostasy in the Qurʾān. The punishment is left to God in the hereafter:

> Glorified be the Lord of the heavens and the earth, the Lord of the Throne, beyond what they describe. So leave them to blunder and play, until they encounter their Day which they are promised. (43, 82–83). See also (42, 70).

In some cases, the Qurʾān mentions some detailed answers to specific insults:

> Among the Jews are those who pervert words from their meanings and say, "We hear and disobey and hear without listening! and *rāʿinā*," twisting their tongues and reviling the faith. But had they said, "We hear and obey and listen and *ʿunẓurnā*," it would have been better for them and more upright. But God has cursed them for their faithlessness, so they will not believe except a few. (4, 46)

Here we do not find silence as an answer; we instead find word against word: do not say this but say that, do not say *rāʿinā* but say *ʿunẓurnā*, which are two synonyms in Arabic that mean "take care of us." However, the first expression, *rāʿinā*, means in Hebrew "our evil one," the word *Raʿ* indicates an Egyptian deity, the supreme deity of the sun, who has become synonym of Satan in Hebrew. Of course, all of this must not be an excuse to claim an anti-Jewish attitude. The verses speak of a specific group of Medinan Jews at the time of the Prophet.

On many occasions, the Qur᾿ān mentions the insults that the Prophet Muḥammad suffered, called by his people a madman, sorcerer, liar:

> Your companion is not mad (or possessed). (81, 22). See also (6, 15), (27, 26), (37, 36), (44, 14), (51, 39 , 52), (52, 29), (54, 9), (68, 2, 51).

Despite the insult, the Prophet is named "companion" and not the enemy of the people who insulted him. The only human emotion understandable in case of insult, expressed by the Prophet, was sadness and not anger. He felt sad because he thought he had not done enough to convey the message, considering the rejection and insult as his failure:

> Do not let their words grieve you. (10, 65), (36, 76). See also (3, 176), (5, 41), (6, 33).

> Perhaps you may destroy yourself with grief, chasing after them, if they do not believe in this discourse. (18, 6). See also (26, 3).

After these considerations, one can legitimately ask: how can we understand that some Islamic law schools, centuries after the death of the Prophet, have chosen the death penalty as a punishment for blasphemy? It is the same case of apostasy, which is absent in the Qur᾿ān and the Prophet's practice. It is a question here of a political vision that saw in blasphemy and apostasy a type of rebellion or a challenge to public order. Since there is nothing in the Qur᾿ān that justifies the death penalty in these cases, jurists have relied on some sayings attributed to the Prophet, which are quite questionable and contradict the Qur᾿ān itself.[73]

Responding to Physical Violence

After seeing the response to verbal violence, let us take a closer look at the Qur᾿ānic response to physical violence. First, it should be emphasized that Islam, like other religions, confirms the sacredness of life:

> Because of that [the story of Cain and Abel], We ordained for the Children of Israel: that whoever kills a person, unless it is for murder or corruption

> on earth, it is as if he killed the whole of mankind; and whoever saves it, it is as if he saved the whole of mankind. (5, 32)[74]

The Qur'ān never justifies offensive war; war can only be defensive and is limited to stopping aggression, as these verses show:

> Fight in the cause of God those who fight you, but do not commit aggression; God does not love the aggressors. (2, 190)

> Fight them until there is no oppression, and worship becomes devoted to God alone. But if they cease, then let there be no hostility except against the oppressors. The sacred month for the sacred month; and sacrilege calls for retaliation. Whoever commits aggression against you, retaliate against him in the same measure as he has committed against you. And be conscious of God and know that God is with the righteous. (2, 193–194)

> If you were to retaliate, retaliate to the same degree as the injury done to you. But if you resort to patience, it is better for the patient. So be patient. Your patience is solely from God. And do not grieve over them, and do not be stressed by their schemes. God is with those who are righteous and those who are virtuous. (16, 126–128)

> If they incline towards peace, then incline towards it, and put your trust in God. He is the Hearer, the Knower. If they intend to deceive you, God is sufficient for you. It is He who supported you with His aid, and with the believers. (8, 61–62)

In extreme cases of aggression against the community, reacting to violence with violence is allowed under certain conditions:

- To be a legitimate defense.
- To be proportionate and not exaggerated.
- To stop at the first sign of peace.
- Patience and non-reaction are recommended.

The Qur'ānic realistic pacifism does not exclude the horizon of radical nonviolence, as we will see later in the Qur'ānic narratives. Nonviolence remains the norm for individual behavior. However, for social and political conduct, we should wait for the Gandhian moment in the twentieth century to testify a radical Islamic nonviolence as a political vision, as we will see later in the historical narratives. "Islamic empires"[75] is a contradictory term, as are today's "Democratic empires" and colonial powers.

CHAPTER TWO

The Qur'ānic Narratives

The Qur'ānic narratives, that is, the stories of the Prophets, *qaṣaṣ al-anbiyā'*, are of the highest importance not only for the fact that they represent more than a quarter of the entire Qur'ānic text,[1] but especially for their rich mythical and symbolic nature, appreciated and elaborated by the Sufis and often neglected by the theologians and jurists.

The stories of the Qur'ān can be a source for a narrative theology that gives more colors and humanistic dimensions to the theory. Classical Islamic theology, Kalām, like its Christian counterpart, often uses philosophical and abstract discourse. A positive evaluation of the stories and "myths" in the Qur'ān could help to rediscover the original religious language, which is simpler and closer to the richness of the religious experience itself. It is a discourse that could be understood by all, each according to his or her spiritual and cultural levels of understanding, in which diversity of levels does not mean necessarily contradiction. These levels of understanding begin with an evident meaning and arrive at symbolic and hidden ones, which contain vast nuances. Studying profoundly the spiritual meaning of these stories is a journey laden with experience and wisdom.

This chapter delves into a series of stories that confirm and develop the nonviolent principles discussed in the first chapter. We deal successively with some ambiguous stories that do not at first glance fit into nonviolent logic to find other interpretative possibilities. This study does not claim to be inclusive, but the examples give a broad vision and complete the theory with new elements.

Nonviolent Narratives

The Meaning of Being Human

At the beginning, I would like to analyze a series of stories that are the *mythical* foundation of Qur'ānic anthropology. These stories consider violence not only as an immoral act but also as an existential element with different facades and forms, rooted in the innate nature of the human being.

I start from the presupposition that the main role, I would say the religious role of religion, is to free the human being from the prison of egoism, both individual and collective. In these two levels of egoism one finds the origin of violence: the negation of the other as a person or as a group. Religion should be a liberator and educator of free men and women, because it is not possible to meet God and fellow human beings with the egoistic veil of separation. Unfortunately, human history in general and the history of religions in particular are full of every type of violence and dominance. It is legitimate to ask: Who really is this violent being called "man"? What is his existential reality? What is his role and mission in life and history? The role of religion is, indeed, to meditate and reflect on these perennial questions.

The following Qur'ānic verses on the creation of Adam, archetype of the human being, will help us understand a part of the Islamic answer:

> When your Lord told the angels, "I am putting a vicegerent [*khalīfa*] on earth." They said, "How can You put someone there who will cause corruption in it and shed blood, when we celebrate Your praise and proclaim Your holiness?" He said, "I know things you do not." He taught Adam all the names, then He showed them to the angels, and said, "Tell Me the names of these, if what you say be true." They said, "May You be glorified! We have knowledge only of what You have taught us. You are the All Knowing and All Wise." Then He said, "Adam, tell them the names of these." When he told them their names, God said, "Did I not tell you that I know what is hidden in the heavens and the earth, and that I know what you reveal and what you conceal?" (2, 30–33)

The title of honor given to this new creature *khalīfa*, which could be translated as "vicegerent," "vicar," "successor," "deputy," or "representative of God," is the first element that attracts attention to these verses. The *khalīfa* realizes and actualizes the moral Will of God and guarantees harmony and unity in the world; it is for this reason that the human being was created. The vicegerent is not the owner of a property but the one responsible for it in the name of the real Owner, who appointed him. He is the representative who does the Will of God, who sent him. The Will of God is none other than the safeguarding of Creation, by respecting its innate equilibrium and participating in the harmony of the cosmic symphony.

Theologically speaking, the divine Will has two levels: cosmic and ethical. The cosmic level, where everything is submitted to God, means being *muslim* in the widest and most general sense of the word; while the ethical and moral Will is realized through the human being and his or her free will, which includes the possibility of rebellion, disharmony, and violence. This is the paradox and the dilemma of human existence: the guarantee of harmony on earth encompasses the freedom to do the contrary.

In the protest of the angels we find the expression "corruption in it," that is, in earth, when they asked, "How can You put someone there who will cause corruption in it and shed blood?" There is a strong correlation here between the violence of a human being against his fellow beings and violence against nature. This multidimensional violence is called "the corruption of the earth," in the Qur'ān.[2] The term "corruption" includes all types of the violence of imbalance and disharmony provoked by the human being.

There are many verses in the Qur'ān that confirm the "original" human weakness:

> No! [But] indeed, man transgresses; because he sees himself self-sufficient. (96, 6–7)

> Indeed, we offered the Trust to the heavens and the earth and the mountains, and they declined to bear it and feared it; but man [undertook to] bear it. Indeed, he was unjust and ignorant. (33, 72)

> God intends to lighten our burden, for the human being was created weak. (4, 28)

> Man was truly created anxious [restless, impatient]. (70, 19)

These verses indicate the complex nature of the human being, as well as his or her grandeur and limit. On the one hand, he is ambitious and worthy of God because of God's Spirit breathed into him; on the other hand, he is full of weakness and interior obstacles. It is the dilemma of human existence, as we have already mentioned. The observation of the angels was partial, but not totally false. Half-truth is falsity, in other words.

Every creature has its place and function in Creation, except the human being, who, because he has free will, can be better than the angels or worse than the animals. Corruption, distraction, or imbalance are works of the human being. Only man is capable of this, as the Qurʾān affirms:

> Corruption has appeared throughout the land and sea by [reason of] what the hands of people have earned so He may let them taste part of [the consequence of] what they have done that perhaps they will return [to righteousness]. (30, 41)

This dangerous potential created fear in the angels, who said: "How can You put someone there who will cause corruption and shed blood, when we celebrate Your praise and proclaim Your holiness?" They saw only the apparent fragility in the composition of the human being, or rather the clay, without noticing his hidden dimension, his mystery, the divine Spirit. They limited themselves to the appearance of human nature and guessed the expected history, which seems to be never ending war and violence, a history of domination and power. Corruption and violence are completely and radically opposed to angelic praise and the hidden history, absent in books written by triumphant kings. It is the history of simple and humble people, a history of love and sainthood, which is the true *raison d'être* for the creation of humanity. At that moment, the angels could not predict the other possibility.

What must be noted, aside from stupefaction is, I would say, the protest of the angels! The angels are pure and obedient creatures, but one intuits they also have a critical spirit. Their judgment is based on the nature of Adam foreseeing the future history of mankind. One can be critical even in the realm of angels! It is a kind of critique inserted into a dialogical context. This scene shows dialogue as divine pedagogy: dialogue between God and the angels, God and Satan, God and Adam. Adam, here, is the symbol of mankind, the primordial prototype that includes Eve, before sex and gender.

This duality and tension or sometimes oppositional complementarity in Adam's composition could be seen as internal and external at the same time:

- The primordial Adam = clay + the Spirit of God
- The primordial Adam = Eve + Post-Eve Adam
- The primordial Adam = Cain + Abel

The verses mentioned above highlight the power of the names given to Adam, a cognitive power that allows him to exercise his role as vicegerent of God in charge of the earth. Adam, due to his forgetfulness and fragility, but also because of his pride and egoism, often risks losing his proper vision and position when he fails to give the right names to things. Adam fell into this play of words, when Satan made him believe that the tree of Paradise is a fountain of life and eternal power. Saying the true names is an act of justice, which guarantees the equilibrium between reality and thought, between the interior world and what surrounds the human being. In the confusion and the absence of a logical order of names and values, ethics become meaningless, everything becomes hypothetically possible, where all are equal. Adam loses his power when he uses it in a negative way, resulting in his no longer knowing how to use it. Instead, he listens to Satan.

> Satan whispered to Adam, saying, "Adam, shall I show you the tree of immortality and power that never decays?" (20, 120)

Knowing Adam's needs and ambitions, his ideas and natural weakness, Satan uses false names by attributing imaginary and magic powers to the tree, in order to cause Adam's fall. Satan's games rely on changing and falsifying names, creating confusion and chaos.

With the use of abusive and deceiving words, the human being tries to conceal the scandal, or, worse still, tries to beautify an ugly reality to make it acceptable. Today, in the name of progress, development, and growth, the earth is devastated by egoistical and imperialistic projects which perceive nature as a prey that has to be exploited and used to its last drop of life.

We can therefore say that false names and lies are the roots of violence. Who succumbs to violence calls it by its real name, although the aggressor never calls it violence. He employs names which have connotations of honor and value, and which purport to advocate democracy or to civilize the world. In the economic sphere, one hears words like "development," "growth," "investments," and so forth . . . No one in the system dares to pronounce their real names of "exploitation," "abuse," "slavery," "speculation," and "usury." The aggressors use a satanic word game to justify violence and thus deceptively embellish what they do. Lying is verbal violence, which is easily transformed into psychological violence, which subsequently escalates into physical violence.

Protest and Rebellion

In the second scene, the story of the creation of Adam continues:

> Your Lord said to the angels, "I will create a man from clay. When I have shaped him and breathed from My Spirit into him, bow down before him." The angels all bowed down together, but not Iblīs, who was too proud. He became a rebel. God said, "Iblīs, what prevents you from bowing down to what I have created with My own hands? Are you too high and mighty?" Iblīs said, "I am better than him: You created me from fire, and You created him from clay." "Get out of here! You are rejected: My rejection will follow you till the Day of Judgement!" (38, 71–78)

The sin of Iblīs is by nature egoistical: "I am better than him," and racist: "You created me from fire, and You created him from clay." Iblīs believed in the nobility and superiority of his nature and race; racism is the first sin. Iblīs's pride made him see the other as a potential enemy who could threaten his position and his presumed supremacy, a rival to be eliminated. So, with his witty use of nominalism, Iblīs deceived Adam, as he believed in the stupidity and mediocrity of the human being. Violence usually starts from the idea of inequality and racism.

God accepted the angels' protests, but not that of Iblīs. The angels also protested against the creation of such a violent creature, but their protest was in the form of a question asked in humility and sincerity; they desired to learn and to know. The protest of Iblīs, however, was more of a challenge, born of pride and rebellion.

In the Sufi tradition, it is said that Iblīs used a pious justification for his rebellion, saying: I cannot adore a creature. I am faithful to the Lord. I cannot bow down before a creature.[3] However, this is a religious justification for racism, making one feel more regal than the king, more faithful to God than God himself. It is a rebellion masquerading as obedience. This satanic zeal is present in some religious milieu, where form becomes more important than the spirit and essence, as indicated in the oath taken by Iblīs: "I swear by Your Might! I will tempt all but Your true servants." (38, 82–83). Iblīs vowed to deceive all the children of Adam: it is hatred in the name of God for all humanity, he swore by God's Might. It is religious racism. Our egoistic understanding of God's Will, which becomes more important than the divine Will itself, is a veil and an idol. Discovering the Will of God, instead, is a process that goes beyond our private interest. The angels were ready to change idea and position in their questioning. Iblīs was not able to change himself; he left with the same position with which he entered, pride and arrogance.

The First Fratricide

The third scene describes the first crime of fratricide on earth, the prototype of bloody violence. The protagonists remain anonymous, called by a common name "Adam's two sons." All of us are the children of Adam, *banū Ādam*:

> [O Prophet], tell them the truth about the story of Adam's two sons: each of them offered a sacrifice, and it was accepted from one and not the other. One said, "I will kill you," but the other said, "God only accepts the sacrifice of those who are mindful of Him. If you raise your hand to kill me, I will not raise mine to kill you. I fear God, the Lord of all worlds, and I would rather you were burdened with my sins as well as yours and became an inhabitant of the Fire: such is the evildoers reward." But his soul prompted him to kill his brother: he killed him and became one of the losers. God sent a raven to scratch up the ground and show him how to cover his brother's corpse and he said, "Woe is me! Could I not have been like this raven and covered up my brother's body?" He became remorseful. On account of [his deed], We decreed to the Children of Israel that

> if anyone kills a person—unless in retribution for murder or for spreading corruption in the land—it is as if he kills all mankind, while if any saves a life it is as if he saves the lives of all mankind. Our messengers came to them with clear signs, but many of them continued to commit excesses in the land. (5, 27–32)

In this scene, one sees man with his desires and contradictions, but strangely enough, Satan is totally absent, in spite of the dominant presence of the satanic model of religious jealousy. *Al-qurbān*, the sacrifice, from which the verb *qarraba* is derived, from the root *q.r.b.*, means to come closer. Therefore *qurbān,* which means an act of coming closer to God, has become the symbol of discord, of sin, of distance from God. It has become the reason for jealousy, violence, and homicide. It is a metaphor for religion, which is supposed to lead to God. But instead, in former as well as in contemporary times, it is often used to justify war and religious jealousy, or what is known in theological terms as "exclusivism."

The key phrase "If you raise your hand to kill me, I will not raise mine to kill you," which is totally absent in the Bible, means refusal of violence and, at the same time, its condemnation and denunciation. This could serve as the theological basis for peaceful struggle against injustice and a possible current of nonviolence originating from the Qurʾān. Nonviolence does not mean assuming a lax attitude, or a weak acceptance of destiny and violence. On the contrary, it is a courageous choice that has its fruits in the penitence of the aggressor brother. The story of the repentant man, our own story, begins with man's return to the tenderness of nature, as he notices the raven, a bird usually considered ugly. The violence of man is an imbalance in the cosmic harmony, and penitence is the return to the initial state of peace and harmony. Violence is blind, but repentance and the return toward God result in a new cosmic awareness. When man reopens his eyes to discover the signs of God, they will indicate the way to peace. Even a raven can be a great master!

In this story, there are two elements: the refusal of the victim to imitate the aggressor, and the imitation of the killer of the innocent victim. The cure for violence, in this vision, is to cut the chain of reactions of mimetic violence, by creating an alternative mimetic model of peace.

Penitence is better understood as the recovery of unity and harmony with creation, as found in reading these verses about "the cosmic prayer" and "the saint's prayer":

> The seven heavens and the earth and whatever is in them exalt Him. And there is not a thing except that it exalts [God] by His praise, but you do not understand their [way of] exalting. Indeed, He is ever forbearing and forgiving. (17, 44)

> And We certainly gave David from Us bounty. [We said], "O mountains, repeat [Our] praises with him, and the birds [as well]." And We made pliable for him iron. (34, 10)

In the last verse, we find a magnificent encounter between the praise of God and industry, between faith and engineering, as represented by the malleability of iron, an encounter still missing in our modern globalized world. David, the psalmist, a symbol uniting Jews, Christians, and Muslims, represents wisdom and prophecy for a united and harmonious world, hindering iron's strong impact in subduing the songs of the mountains and the birds. In this context David is the symbol of the universal human being, called *khalīfa* in the Qurʾān, as was Adam:

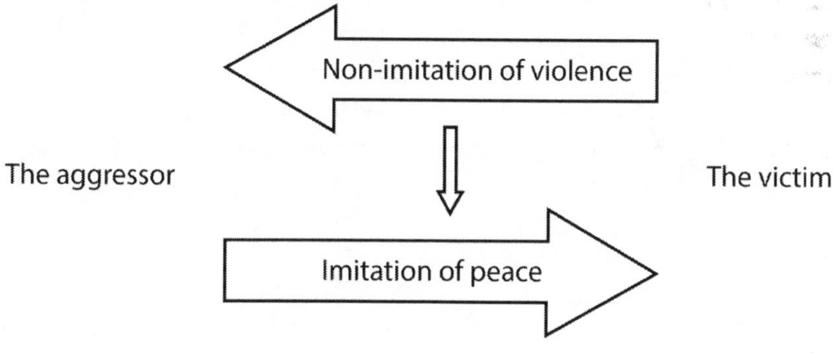

FIGURE 1. Inverted mimetism in the story of Adam's two sons

> O David, We made you a *khalīfa* in the land, so judge between the people with justice, and do not follow desire, lest it diverts you from God's path. (38, 26)

The radical and extreme attitude of the innocent victim, refusing to react to the violence and risking his life, is expressed in more subtle way as an ethical principle in these verses:

> O you who believe! Be upright to God, witnessing with justice; and let not the hatred of a certain people prevent you from acting justly. Adhere to justice, for that is nearer to piety; and fear God. God is informed of what you do. God has promised those who believe and work righteousness: they will have forgiveness and a great reward. (5, 8–9)

> Good and evil cannot be equal. Repel evil with what is better and your enemy will become as close as an intimate friend, but only those who are steadfast in patience, only those who are blessed with great righteousness, will attain to such goodness. If a prompting from Satan should stir you, seek refuge with God: He is the All Hearing and the All Knowing. (41, 33–36)

The message here is that the good is the best way to respond to evil and bad deeds, and that evil's success in transforming us in its image has not been achieved. Reacting to evil with the good could be an opportunity for the aggressor to repent and to imitate the good.

The answer to bad imitation, *sunna sayyi'a*, is good imitation, *sunna ḥasana*, which are two well-known terms in the prophetic Tradition.[4] The solution for jealousy and rivalry is "to compete in good deeds," as confirmed by many verses (2, 148), (5, 48), and as explained in the first chapter. Qur'ānic pedagogical methodology recognizes human instincts and nature, and tries to orient them to a positive and safe end.

Abraham's Sacrifice

The story of Abraham's sacrifice is narrated only once in the Qur'ān, in sūra 37, al-Ṣāffāt. The Islamic Tradition offers further details. The Qur'ānic version is the following, placed in its broad context:

> Of his kind [Noah] was Abraham. When he came to his Lord with a sound (pure) heart. He said to his father and his people, "What are you worshiping? Is it falsified gods, instead of God, that you want? So what is your opinion about the Lord of the worlds?" Then he took a glance at the stars. And said, "I am sick." But they turned their backs on him, and went away. Then he turned to their gods, and said, "Will you not eat? What is it with you, that you do not speak?" Then he turned on them, striking with his right hand. And they came running towards him. He said, "Do you worship what you carve? When God created you, and what you manufacture?" They said, "Build a pyre for him, and throw him into the furnace." They wished him ill, but We made them the losers.
>
> He said, "I am going towards my Lord, and He will guide me." "My Lord, give me one of the righteous." So We gave him good news of a clement boy.
>
> Then, when he was old enough to accompany him, he said, "O my dear son, I see in a dream that I am sacrificing you; see what you think." He said, "O my father, do as you are commanded; you will find me, God willing, one of the steadfast." Then, when they had submitted, and he put his forehead down. We called out to him, "O Abraham! You have fulfilled the vision." Thus We reward the doers of good. This was certainly an evident test. And We redeemed him with a great sacrifice. And We left with him for later generations. Peace be upon Abraham. Thus We reward the doers of good. He was one of Our believing servants. And We gave him good news of Isaac, a prophet, one of the righteous. And We blessed him, and Isaac. But among their descendants are some who are righteous, and some who are clearly unjust to themselves. (37, 83–113)

It is important to read the story of Abraham's sacrifice in its broad context, considering the previous passage. The sacrifice story comes immediately after the confrontation between Abraham and his people, which ends with the destruction of the idols and the aggressive reaction of the people who threw him into the fire, but God saved him. The connection between the two episodes is Abraham's prayer:

> He said, "I am going towards my Lord, and He will guide me." "My Lord, give me one of the righteous." So We gave him good news of a clement boy. (37, 99–101)

It is a prayer that includes two elements: a supplication for guidance accompanying his immigration, Abraham's Hegira, and a request to have a child, which was fulfilled a few years later. This prayer explains the link between Abraham's exit from the city of Ur, abandoning his people's idols, and the subsequent sacrifice. The sacrifice concretely shows Abraham's seriousness in abandoning pagan worship. He destroyed the external idols, risking his life; he also had to destroy the internal idols, the ghosts of the soul, and his father's unconscious inheritance. The firstborn's sacrifice was a Mesopotamian practice of the time,[5] and it was still present in Abraham's mind. The Qur'ān does not speak of Abraham's nightmare but of a divine vision that ordered him to sacrifice his son. God wanted to put Abraham to the test to free him from any trace of the past. For this reason, the Sufis have interpreted that story as a sacrifice of the ego, the great idol, the beloved inner child that we make grow to become a giant.

Another essential element in the Qur'ānic narrative, absent from the Bible, is the son's consent, who was mature enough to decide to participate in the sacrifice. It was also "the sacrifice of the son." Some commentators of the Qur'ān ask if the test was more challenging for the son or the father.[6] Some say that despite the consent, the son suffered more because he did expect love and tenderness from his father. This contradiction is summed up in Abraham's declaration: "O my dear son, I see in a dream that I am sacrificing you" (37, 102). A juxtaposed tenderness and cruelty.[7]

The Qur'ānic story does not reveal the son's name, but it is understood that it is Ishmael, considering the sequence of good news: "So We gave him good news of a clement boy" (37, 101), before the sacrifice. And then "and We gave him good news of Isaac, a prophet, one of the righteous" (37, 112), immediately after the sacrifice and redemption. Isaac seems to be the reward for Abraham's faithfulness, the children's blessing after the trial. One must lose everything to receive in abundance.

So why did the Qur'ān choose to hide Ishmael's name? Perhaps it wanted to avoid a useless detail to emphasize the most important aspect of sacrifice, which symbolically and spiritually means the ego's annihilation. The rivalry between Ishmael and Isaac—first between their mothers Hagar and Sarah, and subsequently between Islam and Judaism—must not disturb the ultimate goal of the story, which goes beyond all rivalries and surpasses them all.

The Muslim reader knows that the story implicitly speaks of Ishmael; this fact is engraved in the Arab memory and in the Islamic Tradition, which sees

Abraham and Ishmael as the founders of Mecca's temple, the Kaʿba. Sacrifice was the spiritual preparation for the foundation. The Temple of God rises on the emptiness of man. The rituals of the pilgrimage to Mecca are a symbolic reproduction of the story of Abraham. His sacrifice is represented by Satan's stoning, who tempted Abraham, trying to discourage him from making the sacrifice. Satan here is a humanist; he tries to convince Abraham of the sacredness of life: "You are crazy! You want to kill your son!" Satan is also the internal voice in the human soul that pushes him toward attachment, in Buddhist terms, against all liberation. This ritual is done three days in three places, throwing small stones against a pillar to relive Abraham's resistance to repetitive temptation.

In truth, it was not the first sacrifice that Ishmael has known: years before, he and his mother suffered exclusion, risking their lives in the desert. We find a Qur'ānic reference to this episode:

> "Our Lord, I have settled some of my offspring in a valley of no vegetation, by Your Sacred House, our Lord, so that they may perform the prayers. So make the hearts of some people incline towards them, and provide them with fruits, that they may be thankful." (14, 37)

The Tradition comments on the verse with a long story:

> Ibn ʿAbbās narrates: "Ibrāhīm [Abraham] brought the mother of Ismāʿīl [Ishmael] and her son, Ismāʿīl, whom she was suckling, and left her by the House near a large tree above Zamzam at the highest point of the masjid. At the time, no one resided in Makkah and there was no water. He left them there with a bag of dates and a water-skin. Ibrāhīm then turned and began to leave on the path he had come. The mother of Ismāʿīl followed him and asked: "O Ibrāhīm! Where are you going, leaving us in a valley where there is no companionship or anything else?" She repeated the question several times but he paid no attention to her. She asked: "Has Allah ordered you to do this?" He replied: "Yes." She said: "In that case, He will not allow harm to come to us," and went back. Ibrāhīm continued until he reached al-Thaniyya, where they could not see him. He turned towards the House and supplicated, raising his hands: "Our Lord, I have settled some of my offspring in a valley of no vegetation, by Your Sacred House, our Lord, so that they may perform the prayers. So make the hearts of some people

> incline towards them, and provide them with fruits, that they may be thankful." (14, 37)
>
> The mother of Ismail continued suckling Ismāʿīl and drinking from the water until it was depleted. She was thirsty and her son was thirsty. She looked at him twisting about—or rolling around—and then walked away as she could not endure looking at him. She noticed that Mt. Ṣafā was the closest mountain to her, so she went towards it and climbed it, facing the valley to see if she could see anyone. But she could see no one. She descended from Mt. Ṣafā and when she reached the valley, she raised the edge of her garment and ran like a person in distress until she crossed the valley. She then came to Mt. Marwa, climbed to the top of it to see if she could see anyone. But she saw no one. She did this seven times. Ibn ʿAbbās said: The Messenger of God said: "This is why people run between these two mountains." While looking out from Mt. Marwa, she heard a sound and said, "Shh," to herself to listen more attentively. Again she heard the sound and she said: "You made me hear your sound, but can you also offer any help?" Suddenly, an angel appeared at the spot of Zamzam. He dug the ground with his heels or his wings until water appeared. She gathered the water with her hands into a pond and began scooping it into the water-skin. It continued gushing forth each time she scooped . . . Ibn ʿAbbās said: The Messenger of God said: "May God be merciful to the mother of Ismāʿīl. If she had left Zamzam—or had she not scooped out the water—it would have been a flowing stream." He continued, She drank and suckled her child and the angel said to her: "Do not fear any harm, as a House will be built here for God by this child and his father. God will not allow any harm to come to His people."[8]

The story continues with Ishmael and Hagar's settlement (Hagar is not mentioned by name) after the arrival of an Arab tribe, Jurhum, who chose to settle due to the water. Thus was born the city of Mecca. The story tells of Ishmael's growth and marriage to a woman of the same adoptive tribe, then the death of his mother. Oddly, there is no reference to the sacrifice mentioned in the verses (37, 100–111). However, the second sacrifice could occur after the father's return to Mecca; the pilgrimage's rituals confirm this possibility.

The close relationship between the pilgrimage rituals and Abraham's two sacrifices is noted in the long ḥadīth, as the Prophet says: "This is why people run between these two mountains." It is the ritual called saʿy, running, in which pilgrims imitate Hagar in her anguish and search for salvation, avoiding watching her son dying before her eyes. At a certain moment, she hears a voice, which was initially covered by the cry of a frightened mother, and so she said to herself, "Shh," to better listen to the voice of salvation.

Unlike the biblical story, the decision to send Hagar and Ishmael away in the Qur'ān was not the fruit of Sarah's jealousy;[9] instead, a divine Will revealed to Abraham, as will happen in the next sacrifice. The two sacrifices were willed by God and were made in a saving and redemptive way. God's goal is not to kill but to offer life and good. This saving Will, as Girard well explained, contradicts and disproves the pagan thirst for blood.

Animal sacrifice is obligatory during the great pilgrimage, Ḥajj, which takes place once in a lifetime, recommended for the rest of the Muslims who celebrate the sacrifice simultaneously elsewhere. There is a ritual act that comes immediately after the sacrifice which is the haircut, totally or partially in a symbolic way (women do it only in a symbolic way):

> It was narrated that Anas b. Mālik said: "the Messenger of God stoned the *Jamra*, offered his sacrifice and shaved his head."[10]

This ḥadīth shows the sequence of pilgrimage rituals related to Abraham's sacrifice: the stoning of Satan, the sacrifice of an animal, the cutting of hair. This cutting of the hair is also made on the occasion of the newborn sacrifice, *ʿAqīqa*, as we see in this ḥadīth:

> According to Mālik, Jaʿfar b. Muḥammad reported that his father said, "Fāṭima, the daughter of the Messenger of God, weighed the hair of each of her children, Ḥasan, Ḥusayn, Zaynab, and Umm Kulthūm, when they were born. Then she gave in charity the silver equivalent of the weight of the child's hair."[11]

An animal sacrifice can easily be linked to Abraham's story, but what does hair cutting mean? It would indicate that instead of cutting the son's throat, they cut their hair, which is part of the body, of the self. Animal sacrifice reminds us of Abraham's sacrifice by imitation. However, the haircut reminds us of the gesture's personal and symbolic meaning, seen as an act of self-purification and ego-cutting. In both cases, the sacrifices are always aimed at charity and social solidarity with the poor and family members. The sacrifice itself is not salvific, but obedience and submission to the divine Will, the helping of the poor, really are salvific, because they purify the soul from the ego and educate it to generosity and gratuitousness. For these reasons, Islam is a post-sacrificial religion par excellence, as explained in the first chapter.

Joseph and His Brothers

Joseph's story is one of the most beautiful narratives, as the Qurʾān itself describes it: "We narrate to you the most beautiful of stories" (12, 3). There is no space to quote it entirely; we focus only on the story's nonviolent nature. It is one of many stories that tell the Prophets' suffering with their people, as we saw earlier in Abraham's story, as well as their patience and peaceful reactions against offenses. This one is more dramatic because it tells the brothers' betrayal, referring to Adam's two sons, but the victim here does not die; he survives to tell the rest of the story differently. We can summarize the story through its geometric structure, which has the shape of a mirror according to the rhetorical analysis:[12]

The center in the rhetorical analysis is of particular importance at the semantic level and the hierarchy of ideas. The center of the story is Joseph's speech in prison (F, F′), which can be considered as a single sequence called (X). The core of the story lies between two opposite wings or sub-sections: the part of abandonment, *takhallī*, and trial, *ibtilāʾ*, on the one hand; and the part of manifestation, *tajallī*, and elevation on the other. The abandonment was double: that of the blood family (brothers), and then that of the adoptive family (al-ʿAzīz, the biblical Potiphar, and his wife). These two abandonments are marked by injustice and violence; their symbol is successively the well and the prison. In the second part of the story, we find the manifestations, the glorious moments in Joseph's life: the declaration of his innocence, his rise to power, the reconciliation with the adoptive family, then the reconciliation with the blood family. The first dream, at the beginning of the sūra, finds its concrete interpretation in the end.

Joseph's speech in prison offers the key to understand the whole story: faith in the One God, *tawḥīd*, implies belonging to Him alone. God is faithful; He does not abandon the victim; God was with Joseph in the solitude of the well and the prison's suffering. In solitude, we meet God. Sincere faith in God's Oneness is realized through abandonment and submission to Him, which leads to the manifestation of God on the one hand and that of the *risen* victim. At that moment, Joseph was able to interpret the Pharaoh's dream; his eyes opened to the divine mysteries that he could not see before, as he asked his father to interpret his first dream. The fire of trial has ripened his soul and opened his eyes.

In his manifestation and success, Joseph did not react with violence; he did not avenge anyone; on the contrary, he responded to evil with good and love. Joseph's generosity has no boundaries; his attitude is the ethical realization of the profound meaning of faith in the One God, *tawḥīd*, and submission to His Will, *islām*, as a way of life. There is no more conflict inside the soul, neither bitterness nor sadness; the soul is fully pacified and satisfied. Nonviolence, in this sense, is a spiritual vision of the hidden meaning of life

A Prologue	12, 1–3
B Vision of Joseph	4–7
C Problem of Joseph with his brothers: the trickery of the brothers against Joseph	8–18
D Relative promotion of Joseph	19–22
E Attempted seduction of Joseph by a woman	23–34
F Joseph in prison, interpreter of the visions of two prisoners and prophet of monotheism	35–42
F' Joseph in prison, interprets the vision of the king	43–49
E' Denouement of the seduction by the woman: Joseph rehabilitated	50–53
D' Definitive promotion of Joseph	54–57
C' Problems of Joseph with his brothers: the trickery of Joseph against his brothers	58–98
B' Accomplishment of the vision of Joseph	99–101
A' Epilogue	102–111

FIGURE 2. Rhetorical analysis of the story of Joseph

behind appearances and facades. The opposite of faith in the One God is associationism, *shirk*, which implies the conflict of desires and passions; it is a negative pluralism, in the sense of division and fragmentation, as is evident in Joseph's brothers' case. Associationism also means the deception of the appearance of worldly life and the distraction from the supreme Truth. Violence starts from an internal conflict before becoming an external fact. It is the same way for peace; it is realized inside before manifesting itself outside. Peace is a realized *tawḥīd*. At this level, *tawḥīd* can be understood as a unification of the soul. God does not need to be recognized as One, but by acknowledging His Oneness we unify our souls within each one and among us.

Another essential element in the story is that Joseph, in his forgiveness and nonviolence, was in a power position, which is an additional feature compared with Adam's two sons' story. In Joseph's story, there is a passage from individual ethics to political ethics, in a certain sense. The criticism of the radical nonviolent reading of the verse: "If you extend your hand to kill me, I will not extend my hand to kill you; for I fear God, Lord of the worlds" (5, 28), in the story of Cain and Abel, usually claims that it was only an individual choice, which cannot be political. The story of Joseph adds the political dimension, confirming the nonviolent principle. However, it remains an individual position of a person in power; it is not a collective decision. In the following story, the principle of nonviolence as a political and collective choice through consultation will become more evident.

Ambivalent Narratives

Lot and His Daughters

In the three Abrahamic religions, Lot's story is often used to condemn homosexuality and justify violence and exclusion against gay men.[13] What is evident in the story is the condemnation of violence against strangers, what we today call xenophobia and racism, which sometimes takes the form of rape and sexual abuse. This story is the opposite of Abraham's and Lot's hospitality, a model of how our attitude should be toward the strangers. Paradoxically, the story is sometimes interpreted to justify violence against women, represented by Lot's daughters. On this point, we intercede. The story of the incestuous relationship between Lot and his daughters (Gen. 19, 31–38) is absent in the

TABLE 3. Lot's Story between the Bible and the Qur'ān

The Qur'ān	Genesis
And when Our envoys came to Lot, he was anxious for them, and concerned for them. He said, "This is a dreadful day." And his people came rushing towards him [Lot]; they were in the habit of committing sins. He said, "O my people, *these are my daughters; they are purer for you*. So, fear God, and do not embarrass me before my guests [the angels]. Is there not one reasonable man among you? (11, 77–78). See also (15, 67–71).	. . . the men of Sodom, both young and old, all the people to the last man, surrounded the house; and they called to Lot, "Where are the men who came to you tonight? Bring them out to us, so that we may know them." Lot went out of the door to the men, shut the door after him, and said, "I beg you, my brothers, do not act so wickedly. *Look, I have two daughters who have not known a man*; let me bring them out to you, and do to them as you please; only do nothing to these men, for they have come under the shelter of my roof." (19, 4–8)

Qur'ān. As in the Bible, immediately after they met Abraham, the angels proceeded to Lot's people to destroy them.

The problem, highlighted by Farid Esack,[14] is the paradox, or rather the scandal, of Lot, an "infallible" Prophet and a moral model, offering his daughters to the thug, responding in this way to injustice with another injustice, sacrificing his own daughters to save what seems to be his patriarchal honor, defending his apparently male guests! How can we justify this choice without justifying at the same time women's oppression and marginalization?

The allegorical interpretation could be the solution to avoid embarrassment. So the expression "my daughters" does not mean "my physical daughters" but rather "my spiritual daughters" or "my people's daughters," considering all women of his people as if they were his daughters, a general call to marry the women of the city. This is the position of some commentators of the Qur'ān and the Bible in the past and today.[15]

But if we take "my daughters" literally,[16] can we explore new interpretative possibilities? In this case, Lot's offer could be understood from different and complementary standing points: Lot's offer could be considered as a discourse of panic and survival, in an extremely dangerous situation, it was a matter of death or life! In this case, it is better to lie than to die. Preserving life and safety is prior to telling the truth, a kind of *taqiyya*, dissimulation, permitted in extreme cases of fear and persecution, as mentioned in the Qur'ān, "unless it is to protect your own selves against them" (3, 28). It is the same case of Abraham when he told Pharaoh that Sarah was his sister,[17] or the "blasphemy" of ʿAmmār Ibn Yāsir under torture in Mecca, when the Prophet Muḥammad told him, "if they turn [to torture you], turn [to do it]."[18] In other words, insult me again if necessary; I am interested in your life more than my "honor."

The real threat was for the guests and not for Lot himself. The offer of Lot seems to be a self-sacrifice; he preferred to "sacrifice" his daughters than to sacrifice his guests, the strangers. The strangers, in this case, are *strangely* more protected than the family's members, which were practically Lot's unique believers' community, the unique success that he had in his almost failed mission. What does it mean in Lot's scale of values and priorities? This possible motivation could be appreciated in the Arabic culture of that time; the example of Ḥātim al-Ṭāʾī, the model of the Arab's generosity, who was a Christian, is well known, when he sacrificed his most beloved horse, his faithful companion, to feed his stranger guests because he had no other things to offer! For Lot, the situation is totally different, but the point is the gratuity of a self-sacrifice. Sons and daughters, in a certain traditional point of view, are considered "part" of their parents, somehow like their property. This point of view is expressed by a ḥadīth that says: "You and your wealth belong to your father."[19]

The reference to the son as the symbol of the self and his sacrifice as self-sacrifice is apparent in Abraham's story, especially in the Sufi interpretation. The son's acceptance is explicit in the Qurʾān (37, 102), not in the Bible. So how to interpret the silence of Lot's daughters, both in the Bible and the Qurʾān? Is their silence a sign of consensus? We can imagine a certain "unity" between them, being the unique followers of their father. Did they accept their father's offer like Abraham's son did? Did Lot ask permission from his daughters? The text is silent about this point.[20]

At the same time, we can understand the offer of Lot as a "tactic" to gain time, or better to change the conversation and to interrupt the threatening atmosphere. In other words, it was not a serious proposal, or at least we cannot take it literally.[21] He was in front of an immediate attack of the mob; he should react to stop or to slow down their excited and emotional movement. To get a peaceful and appeasing impact, the reaction should not be of the same nature of the action. Somehow, to avoid the disaster. It is exactly what René Girard could call: interrupting the mimetic circle of violence. The effective or possible victim of violence reacts in a nonviolent way to break the chain of violence, otherwise he will reproduce or confirm the same violence, so it will be no other alternative or escape from the continuous violence.

In the same way, we can understand the teaching of Jesus: "When someone strikes you on your right cheek, turn the other one to him as well" (Mt 5, 39). The Cross itself could be understood in this manner from a Girardian point of view, as mentioned in the first chapter. In the story of the two sons of Adam, Cain and Abel, especially in its Qur'ānic version, the victim chooses the nonviolence: "If you extend your hand to kill me, I will not extend my hand to kill you; for I fear God, Lord of the worlds" (5, 28). In the story of the Queen of Sheba, as we will see later, she sent gifts to Solomon as an answer to his "threatening" letter: "She said: When kings enter a city, they devastate it, and subjugate its dignified people. Thus, they always do. I am sending them a gift, and will see what the envoys bring back" (27, 24–25).

A Prophet, who faces the failure alone, trying to protect his stranger guests, is a symbol of our human fragility and weakness. At the same time, he is a symbol of human grandeur. God's love is very near, even in the most difficult and desperate moments in which we try to use our limited tools to save ourselves. The Prophet is one of us, not an infallible spiritual Superman! This vision can contradict the traditional doctrine of prophecy in classical Islamic theology, Kalām, which believes in the Prophets' infallibility and sinlessness, *'isma*. This doctrine depicts the Prophets in a rigid and idealistic way that does not do justice to their rich and complex humanity. The Prophets are truthful and credible in their transmission of God's revelation, but they remain beautifully human in their limits.

Moses and the Violent Saint

The story of Moses and the Saint is one of the most mystical and esoteric stories of the Qur'ān. The man called in the Qur'ān, the Servant of God, is known in the Tradition as Khiḍr or Khaḍir, the green man. Considered by the Sufis as the archetype of sainthood and masterhood, *walī Allāh*, the friend of God. There is no room here for a detailed analysis.[22] However, what interests us are the Saint's violent acts in the name of God, which are denounced and condemned from an ethical and juridical point of view, represented in the story by Moses. The most shocking one is the killing of the child. These acts are usually attributed to wicked people and not to saints. For that reason, the story is based on a scandal; shocking paradoxes are part of the Sufi pedagogy to liberate the novice from mental habits and narrow visions. Below is the complete text, mentioned once in the Qurʾān in sūra 18, The Cave, which is composed of stories of the same esoteric nature. The sūras 18 and 19, Mary, are the spiritual heart of the Qurʾān:

> Moses said to his servant, "I will not rest until I reach the place where the two seas meet, even if it takes me years!" but when they reached the place where the two seas meet, they had forgotten all about their fish, which made its way into the sea and swam away. They journeyed on, and then Moses said to his servant, "Give us our lunch! This journey of ours is very tiring," and [the servant] said, "Remember when we were resting by the rock? I forgot the fish—Satan made me forget to pay attention to it—and it [must have] made its way into the sea." "How strange!" Moses said, "Then that was the place we were looking for." So the two turned back, retraced their footsteps, and found one of Our servants—a man to whom We had granted Our mercy and whom We had given knowledge of Our own. Moses said to him, "May I follow you so that you can teach me some of the right guidance you have been taught?" The man said, "You will not be able to bear with me patiently. How could you be patient in matters beyond your knowledge?" Moses said, "God willing, you will find me patient. I will not disobey you in any way." The man said, "If you follow me then, do not query anything I do before I mention it to you myself." They travelled on. Later, when they got into a boat, and the man made a hole in it, Moses said, "How could you make a hole in it? Do you want to drown its passengers? What a strange thing to do!" He replied, "Did I not tell you that you would never be able to bear with me patiently?" Moses said, "Forgive me for forgetting. Do not make it too hard for me to follow you." And so they travelled on. Then, when they met a young boy and the man killed him, Moses said, "How could you kill an innocent person? He has not killed anyone! What a terrible thing to do!" He replied, "Did I not tell you that you would never be able to bear with me patiently?" Moses said, "From now on, if I query anything you do, banish me from your company—you have put up with enough from me." And so they travelled on. Then, when they came to a town and asked the inhabitants for food but

were refused hospitality, they saw a wall there that was on the point of falling down and the man repaired it. Moses said, "But if you had wished you could have taken payment for doing that." He said, "This is where you and I part company. I will tell you the meaning of the things you could not bear with patiently: the boat belonged to some needy people who made their living from the sea and I damaged it because I knew that coming after them was a king who was seizing every [serviceable] boat by force. The young boy had parents who were people of faith, and so, fearing he would trouble them through wickedness and disbelief, we wished that their Lord should give them another child—purer and more compassionate—in his place. The wall belonged to two young orphans in the town and there was buried treasure beneath it belonging to them. Their father had been a righteous man, so your Lord intended them to reach maturity and then dig up their treasure as a mercy from your Lord. I did not do [these things] of my own accord: these are the explanations for those things you could not bear with patience." (18, 60–82)

The narrative aims to underline the difference between two levels of the divine Will:

1. The ethical Will, represented by Moses and revealed to him through the Ten Commandments: "Thou shalt not kill" (Ex. 20, 13), which are confirmed by the Qur'ān in many verses, as we saw in the first chapter.
2. The ontological Will, which has a different logic and includes "evil" in its natural forms, such as death and disasters, and in its human forms, such as "criminal" acts. These acts and phenomena, which are bad for us because they damage and harm life, do not represent a cosmic disorder or a satanic rebellion. Indeed, the satanic rebellion is included in this plan; it is allowed and willed by God on the ontological level. It is the same God who orders good and forbids unbelief and injustice at the ethical level.

Divine action moves on a different existential level, which we are often unable to see or understand at first sight, not only because of the veils that cover human vision but also because of the limited time that we have available. Life is short, and it does not often allow us to see finality and teleology. However, we still know by faith that the ethics of divine action is Mercy (6, 54), despite appearances and sufferings. The goal of the story is to arouse an unshakable trust in divine Wisdom. The Saint was so transparent and united with the divine that in the end, he became an aware instrument in the hands of God through a private and intimate knowledge, *ʿilm ladunnī*. It is not the ethical norm but the supra-human Will of God that embraces everything. There is no room for absurdity; in the Realm of Unity, there is no duality nor rivalry—all the contradictions are solved in the One. The story does not offer a model of conduct, but rather a model of thinking, a theological and mystical vision: the divine Will cannot be reduced in human ethics and values, despite that Mercy is the essence of God's actions and Being.

Solomon and the Queen of Sheba

The last story in this series is Solomon and the Queen of Sheba[23] in the sūra of the Ants (27, 15–44), in one narrative block not repeated elsewhere in the Qurʾān. Unfortunately, some commentators used this story to justify violence and men's superiority over women.[24] However, a deep reading can lead us to a different conclusion. Despite the appearance, the story is profoundly nonviolent, like Joseph's story, and not less complex and beautiful.

The story begins with Solomon searching for the hoopoe, threatening to punish him. A threat that was never realized, as other threats in the same story. The hoopoe justified his absence by a discovery:

> I have learned something you did not know: I come to you from Sheba with firm news. I found a woman ruling over the people, *who has been given a share of everything*, she has a mighty throne, [but] I found that she and her people worshipped the sun instead of God. (27, 23–24, the emphasis is mine)

The special characters of the Queen, as described by the hoopoe, shows a strong bond between her and Solomon, as mentioned just a few verses before:

> Solomon succeeded David. He said: "People, we have been taught the speech of birds, and *we have been given a share of everything*; this is clearly a great favor." (27, 16, the emphasis is mine)

Here, the Queen of Sheba is potentially another archetypal figure of relative perfection, out of the line of David and the monotheistic system. It is like discovering another solar system outside our own galaxy, far away, but it looks differently similar. The dichotomy in the Queen's personality is quite clear: on the one hand, she is a wise queen, given a share of everything, just like Solomon, but on the other hand there is a serious defect, the idolatry, the worship of the sun.[25] It is an imperfect perfection. The same imperfect perfection is found in the character of Solomon, but in a more subtle way.[26]

The first reaction of Solomon to the hoopoe's news is to send a message, which seems to be a threat, in order to test her:

> [Solomon] said: "We shall see whether you are telling the truth or lying. Take this letter of mine and deliver it to them, then withdraw and see what answer they send back." [The Queen of Sheba] said: "Counselors, here is delivered to me a letter worthy of respect.[27] It is from Solomon, and it says, 'In the name of God, the Lord of Mercy, the Giver of Mercy, do not put yourselves above me, and come to me in submission.'" She said, "Counselors, give me your counsel in the matter I now face: I only ever decide on matters in your presence." They replied, "We possess great force and power in war, but you are in command, so consider what orders to give us." She said, "Whenever kings go into a city, they ruin it and humiliate its leaders, that is what they do, but I am going to send them a gift, then see what answer my envoys bring back." (27, 27–35)

The Queen, in that initial moment, did not know what she had in common with Solomon; she thought that he could act like any invader, destroying everything in his path. These verses explain the beauty and majesty of the Queen: the consultation, the choice of peace, the use of diplomacy to avoid confrontation, despite the military advice of the male counselors. They are signs of moral strength and female wisdom. The Queen started from the appearance of history to later discover a secret history, the mystical and hidden realities of the world, a king not like the others, a king of feminine soul like her, who avoids crushing the ants for love and mercy:

> And when they came to the Valley of the Ants, one ant said, "Ants! Go into your homes, in case Solomon and his hosts unwittingly crush you."

> Solomon smiled broadly at her words and said, "Lord, inspire me to be thankful for the blessings You have granted me and my parents, and to do good deeds that please You; admit me by Your grace into the ranks of Your righteous servants." (27, 18–19)

There is a similarity between the cry of the "queen" of the ants and the Queen of Sheba. The "official" history of mankind is full of blood and violence, against the fellow humans and against women in particular, and against living beings and nature in general. Solomon, however, was a king who comes from an "other" world, of which there are quite no traces in the books of history.

The Queen made her first diplomatic attempt, by sending a gift to Solomon; perhaps that would deter him—in her opinion—from the attack. Solomon refused the gift, considering it an insult. He does not look for the wealth of people to get rich; God gave him already a share of everything:

> When he [the embassy] came to Solomon, he said, "Are you supplying me with money? What God has given me is better than what He has given you. It is you who delight in your gift. Go back to them. We will come upon them with troops they cannot resist; and we will expel them from there, disgraced and humiliated." (27, 36–37)

Solomon's refusal increased the Queen's fears and suspicions, as the diplomatic attempt failed and was followed by an explicit threat of invasion. Nevertheless, she did not surrender to the logic of war, which at one point seemed to be inevitable. She decided to risk herself and to personally go to meet Solomon, hoping that she might get by direct dialogue what she could not get by sending gifts. It was an act of self-sacrifice for the sake of her nation and kingdom. This bold step is not mentioned explicitly in the text, but it is inferred through context: the meeting place was Solomon's court, which necessitates her displacement. Solomon did not translate his threat into action; he was expecting her to come, as if his apparent threat was merely a provocative invitation.

Arriving to Solomon, she found other tests and surprises waiting for her:

> When she arrived, she was asked, "Is this your *throne*?" She replied, "It looks like it." [Solomon said], "We were given knowledge before her, and we devoted ourselves to God; she was prevented by what she worshipped

> instead of God, for she came from a disbelieving people." Then it was said to her, "Enter the hall (or the palace)," but when she saw it, she thought it was a deep pool of water, and bared her legs. Solomon explained, "It is just a hall paved with glass," and she said, "My Lord, I have wronged myself and I have submitted, with Solomon, to God, the Lord of the worlds." (27, 42–44)

In this context, we find two cases of illusion: considering the true as false, the true throne as an imitation, *ka'annahu huwa*, "It looks like it," literally, "as if this is it"; and the second illusion being considering the false as true, the crystal reflection as water, *ḥasibat-hu lujja*, "she thought it was a deep pool of water." The cause of the illusion could be ignorance, the human condition in general, or the lens of culture, in her case, as the Qur'ān says: "she was prevented by what she worshipped instead of God." It is that point of weakness that was missing in her perfection, and she had to overcome it in the initiation of Solomon; she was veiled by her false belief that prevented her from seeing things as they really are. Mysticism is precisely the capacity of overcoming of the veil, achieving the true vision.

The Queen's final prayer summarizes the goal of the journey. She said, "My Lord, I have wronged myself and I have submitted, with Solomon, to God, the Lord of the worlds." She recognized her limits in an act of penitence and humbleness, submitting to God. We note the expression "with Solomon," and not "to Solomon"; it is not a submission to the person of Solomon, as it seemed at the beginning from the appearance of the letter: "It is from Solomon, and it says: In the name of God, the Lord of Mercy, the Giver of Mercy, do not put yourselves above me, and come to me in submission," (27, 31). The initiation, in this sense, is a passage from the earthly king to the heavenly King, the Lord of the worlds, from Solomon to God, in order to become a "cosmic Queen," a universal man/woman, *insān kāmil*.[28] "With Solomon" is also an act of liberation; the conversion freed her from fear, from the image of the threatening king to discover the tender and friendly king. It marked a new relationship of parity and non-submission, both are equal before God, the Lord of the worlds, the True King. All kingdoms, thrones, powers of the world vanish, only His Face remains (55, 26–27).

The throne is a symbol of power: the parallel/contrast is quite clear between "a mighty throne" of the Queen and the "the mighty Throne" of God, as it is mentioned at the beginning on the hoopoe's tongue:

> I found a woman ruling over the people, who has been given a share of everything, she has *a mighty throne*, [but] I found that she and her people worshipped the sun instead of God. Satan has made their deeds seem alluring to them, and diverted them from the right path: they cannot find the right path. Should they not worship God, who brings forth what is hidden in the heavens and earth and knows both what you people conceal and what you declare? He is God, there is no god but Him, the Lord of *the mighty Throne*.[29] (27, 23–26, the emphasis is mine)

What confirms the parallel between the two mighty thrones is the issue of water:

> It is He who created the heavens and the earth in six days, and *His Throne was upon the waters* . . . (11, 7, the emphasis is mine)

> Then it was said to her, "Enter the hall (or the palace)," but when she saw it, she thought it was a deep pool of *water*, and bared her legs. (27, 42–44, the emphasis is mine)

Bringing the throne from Sheba to Jerusalem is an act of decentralization and relativization. The throne is rigid, fixed, and heavy, symbolizing the strength of centralized power in the hands of the king. This same "center," in our story, becomes "periphery"; it becomes lighter, softer, and, above all, relativized.[30] The initiation here is an act of liberation from the egocentrism, individual and collective, and so the idols and the false absolutes fall down. The falsely worshipped sunlight, "I found that she and her people worshipped the sun instead of God" (27, 24), as the hoopoe described, vanishes, giving way to the true Light: "God is the Light of the heavens and the earth" (24, 35).

The conversion means the invasion and the destruction of ego, only in this sense Solomon's threats were realized. The conversion is an act of elevation and enthronement, when the heart of the believer becomes the Throne of God. Instead of sitting on his or her own egoistic throne, one opens his or her heart to become God's Throne: "The Lord of Mercy [*al-Raḥmān*] established on the Throne" (20, 5).

Another feature of the initiation is its aesthetic and artistic character. The artistic expression, in this case, is of geometric and architectural nature.

The masterpiece of Solomon, the throne in the hall paved with glass, is a physical icon of the metaphysical Truth; "His Throne was upon the waters" (11, 7), an architectural manifestation that reveals the transcendental Invisible in an immanent visible form. It is the same "wonder" that unites the artistic experience and the religious experience. The Queen was converted by wonder and astonishment.[31]

We find in the story of Solomon and the Queen of Sheba the same mechanism underlined previously in the stories of Adam's two sons and Joseph: the will of not imitating the aggressor or what seems to be so. Not to fall into the trap of violence is the first test of initiation to sainthood that opens the eyes to the divine signs. Only in this case she became fully a Queen at the image of King. As for Joseph, the test is an occasion of revelation and elevation, after an apparent destitution that hides the divine Tenderness and Mercy.

CHAPTER THREE

The Historical Narratives

The founding moment in Islamic historical narratives is the biography of the Prophet Muḥammad, Sīra, and his Tradition, Sunna, as found in classical sources. They are an essential reference for understanding Islam as a religion and verifying the application of the Qurʾānic principles and values in historical reality or what is thought to be real. History includes what factually happened in the past and what we think happened, as a collective historical *imaginaire*. In this context, it is necessary to equip oneself with a critical vision to identify the narratives that contradict and betray the Qurʾānic principles and values already explained and commented on in the previous chapters. The Qurʾān represents the supreme reference on the theological level.

The historical narratives include the first centuries and generations of Islamic history: the Companions generation, *Ṣaḥāba*, who were contemporaries of the Prophet and some of whom continued to live after his death; the second generation of the Successors, *Tābiʿūn*; then the third generation of the Successors of the Successors, *Tābiʿū al-tābiʿīn*. The birth of great empires strongly influenced the development of the new community. Islam experienced two moments of foundation: the first was the spiritual foundation with Muḥammad's prophetic mission. The second was the intellectual and scientific foundation, with the birth of Islamic sciences toward the end of the Umayyad era and the beginning of the Abbasid era. This second founding moment has acquired a certain sacredness for many Muslims. Effectively, the second foundation shapes our vision of the first. It was an era of prosperity and glory that marked the collective imagination and the cognitive heritage in terms of ideas and methodologies. Among the difficulties of the reform of Islamic religious thought, today's involve precisely the critical overcoming of the past's epistemological paradigms.

In this context, it is noticeable that some historical narratives contradict the principles of mercy and peace, confirming the "jihadist theory" in the expansionist and imperialist sense. It is a theory born at the Umayyads' time and has developed over the centuries and is still present. It is considered a fundamental religious doctrine that remains until the Last Day. Armed jihadist theory depicts the Prophet's battles as a preparation for the military conquests that occurred after his death. These conquests were conducted effectively by his Successors, then by the Umayyad and Abbasid caliphs and subsequent empires up to the Ottoman Empire. Some ḥadīths, which mention the conquest of Constantinople and Byzantium, are used to justify imperial expansionism:

> Verily, you shall conquer Constantinople. What a wonderful leader will her leader be, and what a wonderful army will that army be![1]
>
> Even if there was only one day left of this world, God would make it last until a man from my household took possession of the mountain of Daylam and Constantinople.[2]

These ḥadīths are considered "weak" by many traditionists of the past and present. There are many doubts about the authenticity of these apocalyptic and eschatological texts, regarding the final battles between good and evil, generally known by traditionists as *aḥādīth al-malāḥim*, "the ḥadīth of the great battles."[3] These texts were used to justify the Ottoman expansions, considering them as a fulfilled prophecy, notably the conquest of Constantinople and the fall of the Byzantine Empire to the hands of Sultan Mehmet I, called the Conqueror, in 1453.

Also significant is the existence of a literary genre, called *al-Siyar wa al-Maghāzī*, literally, "the Biographies and the Expeditions," and sometimes only *al-Maghāzī*, "the Expeditions," which could be among the older Islamic texts.[4] Ambiguously, this genre's very name identifies the Prophet's biography with his battles and military expeditions, as if *al-Siyar* and *al-Maghāzī* were synonymous, or at least as if the latter represented the essential part of the former. Actually, this name is none other than the authors' choice, which expresses their interest in the war part in the Prophet's biography; they were involved in a series of wars known in Islamic history as the "conquests," *futūḥāt*. The military part represented the priority in the historical reading of a particular generation of authors.[5]

In this context, from a religious point of view, only the Prophet's biography is significant, which represents "the good example" (33, 21) for all Muslims. It is an ethical model that must be interpreted in light of the Qur'ān. Meditating on the Sīra, one can understand that the wars that the Prophet waged after he immigrated to Medina were defensive as acts of survival against the attack of an Arab tribal alliance led by Quraysh, the Prophet's tribe. The goal of this extended alliance was precisely to annihilate the Prophet and his nascent community. The Prophet's wars, however, remain faithful to the Qur'ānic theory and the conditions of combat already mentioned:

- To push back the aggression.
- To use the proportionate force.
- To stop fighting as soon as a sign of peace appears.

There is nothing to indicate that the Prophet intended to extend the wars beyond the Arabian Peninsula and the Arab tribal zones. For example, the battle of Mu'ta, in present-day Jordan, in the eighth year of the Hegira, occurred after the killing of ambassadors and missionaries sent by the Prophet to some Arab tribes, the Ghassanids. The fact that these tribes were allied with the Byzantines involved the latter in the conflict. Tabūk's campaign in the ninth year, in present-day Saudi Arabia, which ended without confrontation, is placed in a similar tribal context.

The Ḥudaybiya treaty, in 628, was the turning point in the conflict between the Prophet and his community on the one hand and Quraysh and the allied tribes on the other. According to some Companions, it was a humiliating agreement; it included rejecting Muslims who sought refuge in Medina; meanwhile, Quraysh had the right to receive anyone who denied

Islam and wanted to join Mecca. This agreement had broken the mimetic circle of violence, which was an excellent advantage for Muslims. It introduced a new peaceful logic and applied the already mentioned Qur'ānic principles in a theoretical and narrative way. The treaty saved Muslims from being consumed by a vicious circle of violence and war, which negatively impacted Islam's religious mission and the life of the community. Generalized violence in the Arabian Peninsula prevented the spread of the new faith, a mission that can only be accomplished through peaceful means. On the other hand, the sword creates a reaction of rejection and an atmosphere of hatred and revenge. The objective of the community's survival was not to oppose or cancel the survival of the mission. The call to Islam requires a climate of peace and trust in which one can discuss and speak without fear. The Prophet was aware that war was like a fire that consumes everyone, including his own people, and was astonished at Quraysh's willingness to continue the war. When he went out with his Companions in a peaceful pilgrimage, *'umra*, to Mecca, a little before the treaty, which Quraysh strongly prevented, he said:

> Alas, Quraysh, war has devoured them! What harm would they have suffered if they had left me and the rest of the Arabs to go our own ways?[6]

Ibn Isḥāq, quoting al-Zuhrī, describes the impact of the truce:

> No previous victory in Islam was greater than this [the truce of Ḥudaybiya]. There was nothing but battle when men met; but when there was an armistice and war was abolished and men met in safety and consulted together none talked about Islam intelligently without entering it. In those two years double as many or more than double as many entered Islam as ever before.[7]

Note that the victory, *fatḥ* (sing. of *futūḥāt*), which later took the sense of "conquest," mentioned in the Qur'ānic verse "We have granted you a clear *fatḥ*, victory" (48, 1) refers to the Ḥudaybiya truce, according to many commentators,[8] and not to the conquest of Mecca, as some have thought.

Indeed, the Prophet has won with this truce; otherwise, Mecca's peaceful conquest cannot be understood. The treaty isolated Quraysh and dismantled the tribal alliance through dialogue and diplomacy. Quraysh eventually fell as the last ripe fruit, after all the conditions were in place to end the conflict. The peaceful conquest was concluded with a general amnesty:

> the apostle stood at the door of the Kaʿba [Mecca's temple] and said: . . . "O Quraysh, what do you think that I am about to do with you?" They replied, "Good. You are a noble brother, son of a noble brother." He said: "Go your way for you are the freed ones."[9]

After the conquest of Mecca, all Arabia joined the state of Medina. That year is called "the year of delegations," in which the Arab tribes recognized the religious and political authority of the Prophet Muḥammad. In this way, the Arabian Peninsula was politically unified for the first time, an absolute historical novelty. Aside from southern Arabia (Yemen), the rest have not previously known a central state.

The legitimate question that some ask in this context is: Why did the Prophet forgive his tribe and did not do the same thing with the Jewish tribe of Banū Qurayẓa? It seems that men capable of taking up arms were sentenced to death. Why was the punishment so severe in this case, and there was an amnesty after Mecca's conquest, save for exceptional cases of war criminals?[10]

Indeed, the historical moment was decisive in these choices and decisions. In the case of Banū Qurayẓa, the punishment was applied to "citizens," in modern terms, who had signed the "Constitution of Medina," which included a joint-defense alliance against any attack on the city.[11] Banū Qurayẓa's collaboration with the enemy, the Arab coalition, represented a dangerous betrayal that, if successful, risked exterminating the entire Islamic community. For this reason, the Jewish tribe was punished with the maximum penalty known at the time. The severe punishment represented a warning to all Medinan society members not to fall into the same error.[12] On the other hand, Mecca's general amnesty was in a different context: the end of the war and the foundation of durable peace after excluding any danger or threat. After the conquest of Mecca, no threat was expected from Quraysh, especially after the dissolution of the tribal coalition and after most of the tribes joined the Muslims.

In any case, the extreme, violent punishment raises an ethical dilemma for contemporary Muslims. It is very significant: what once seemed acceptable has now become problematic because of the historical gap. This question creates a moral problem for today's Muslims and puts before them a sensitive question: What does "the good prophetic model" mean today? The great challenge that modern Muslims encounter is fidelity to the Prophet of mercy, considering at the same time the historical distance that separates them from him. Doing that without falling into a literalist reading and without an easy accommodation to modern pressure betrays the text's fundamental values, throwing out the child along with the bathwater. However, the new historical condition requires adopting a different attitude to remain faithful to the same principles established by the Qurʾān. The Prophet's choices were the best ethical choices in his historical context. Today, we should do the same: seek the most suitable moral form of our time, according to our conscience, which is always in the process of development.

The problem is limited not only to the understanding of the Banū Qurayẓa story but also to the conception of defensive warfare in general. Can we rethink defensive warfare conditions in a world filled with weapons of mass destruction and "intelligent" weapons that cannot avoid civilian victims? Let us revisit this crucial question later when we come to the modern era and its challenges.

The Conquests

The historical narratives impose another question: Did the "Islamic" conquests coincide with the Qurʾānic principles? Were the conquests defensive?

The first wars with the Byzantines were in the Arab tribal context, as we have already mentioned. Toward the end of his life, the Prophet decided to send a military expedition under the young Usāma Ibn Zayd leadership to respond to Muʾta's defeat, but his death prevented the expedition. Abū Bakr, who had just become caliph, decided to send the army to punish the rebel Arab tribes. Later on, battles and victories followed, especially with the appearance of military leaders who proved their strategic genius, such as Khālid Ibn al-Walīd, who fought against Muslims in the battle of Uḥud, to become later "the sword of Islam."[13] After the conquest of Egypt, the second caliph, ʿUmar Ibn al-Khaṭṭāb, began to fear this expansionist trend's negative consequences, refusing to extend the military campaign westward (North Africa). His response to General ʿAmr Ibn al-ʿĀṣ, who asked for permission to move forward, was: "No, it is not Ifrīqiyya (Africa), it is rather dispersive, deceived deceiver, no one will go and conquer it as long as I live."[14] It seems that the idea of founding a global empire was not yet firmly rooted.

Persia's conquest, which ultimately led to the Sassanid Empire's fall, was defensively justified in the Islamic sources. The Sassanid king humiliated the Prophet's ambassadors, tearing up the letter they brought and asking his governor in Yemen to arrest Muḥammad or kill him. The governor disobeyed and informed the Prophet. This failed plot was regarded as a declaration of war by the Sassanid Empire. However, the Prophet did not prepare any military campaign to respond to the threats.[15]

It seems that the conquests were the exception that has become the rule. Indeed, they were the exception that reoriented Islamic history, causing a profound change in the nascent community, especially with the accumulation of wealth and treasures transferred from the conquered lands to Medina. The conquests transformed society on all levels, subsequently preparing for the "great discord," *al-fitna al-kubrā*, the first civil war between the Prophet's Companions. The Umayyad Empire, which introduced the hereditarian succession following the Byzantine model, continued the conquests up to China's borders, toward the east, and Andalusia and southern France, toward the west. Thus, the war machine had become an effective instrument of gain and prosperity for the empire through loot and poll taxes. It was also a way to ease internal tensions, in Girardian terms, always searching for an external enemy, a scapegoat, to resolve the internal mimetic rivalry.

These conquests coincided with the abandonment of the principle of consultation and the appearance of hereditarian despotic governments. As a result, violence became the unique way to resolve conflicts between groups that competed for power even within the same family. Thus, Muslims quickly absorbed the empires' political cultures they replaced, perhaps with an Islamic religious veneer, by adopting the jihadist theory, an expansionist ideology, and a military doctrine. This historical and cultural knot is still present in Muslims' thoughts and souls, even after the fall of the last empire and the end of the era of military conquests and glories. We could call this trend "imperialism without empire," which is not limited to nostalgia for the glorious past. This imperialistic dream is not just psychological compensation in the face of the present crises; it is sometimes concretized through terroristic choices that see violence as an absolute priority, as a doctrine that goes beyond time and space. In its modern version among extremist groups, the jihadist theory has become the theory of "perennial war" and "Management of Savagery."[16] It is a war god who has nothing to do with God, which Islam and its Prophet preached. There is a vital need to free ourselves from this knot that has caused significant damage to Islam's image among its people and in the world.

In the historical texts, we find the speech of Rib'ī Ibn 'Āmir, who was a simple soldier in the battle of al-Qādisiyya in the year 636, used to justify the conquest of Persia and the expansionist tendency:

> God has sent us and has brought us here so that we may extricate those who so desire from servitude to the people [here on earth] and make them servants of God; that we may transform their poverty in this world into affluence; and that we may free them from the inequity of the religions and bestow upon them the justice of Islam. He has sent us to bring His religion to His creatures and to call them to Islam. Whoever accepts it from us, we shall be content. We shall leave him on his land to rule it without us; but whoever refuses, we shall fight him, until we fulfill the promise of God . . . We shall therefore go back and leave you alone for three days. Look into your affair and into the affair of your people and choose—within this period—one of three options. Choose Islam, and we shall leave you alone on your land; or choose [to pay] the poll tax, and we shall be content and refrain from fighting you. If you do not need our help, we shall leave you alone; and if you need it, we shall protect you. Otherwise it will be war on the fourth day.[17]

The choices imposed on the religious other were three: to embrace Islam and become one of us, pay the poll tax, *jizya*, or fight to the death. In other words, the other must become in our image, or at least submit to our dominion, or risk exclusion through slavery or death. This approach has marked all the past imperialist tendencies until today—Islamic and non-Islamic, from the Roman age to the Byzantine age and up to modern empires—with different modalities and shades, and sometimes more violently. Today, it is more challenging to justify war by religion. However, other secular justifications are used, such as bringing civilization, prosperity, and democracy; fighting terrorism; or freeing women.

Furthermore, it is noted that the speech attributed to Ribʿī contradicts the Qurʾānic vision expressed in these verses, for example:

> You cannot guide whom you love, but God guides whom He wills, and He knows best those who are guided. (28, 56)

> So remind. You are only a reminder. You have no control over them. (88, 21–22)

Guiding and bringing people out of the darkness into the light is a divine mission that cannot be attributed to men, including the Prophets. This heroic task attributed to man in the speech represents a problematic exaggeration for the faith.

The scandal is that these great victories on the external fronts, at the time of the Umayyads and Abbasids, coincided with the massacres of the Prophet's family on the internal fronts, in Karbalāʾ (year 680) and Fakh (786) and elsewhere, where the descendants of the Prophet were killed and women were taken into captivity. All this while the celebrations of victories and conquests were underway. Many of the founders of law schools suffered imprisonment and torture, and death in some cases, at the hands of the governors of their time, because of their opinions, such as Abū Ḥanīfa (d. 767), Mālik Ibn Anas (d. 795), and Aḥmad Ibn Ḥanbal (d. 855).[18] A more violent treatment was reserved for the great masters of Sufism, such as the killings of Ḥallāj (d. 922) and Suhrawardī (d. 1191). Hither, martyrdom is a nonviolent action in the face of power, which could no longer tolerate opinions other than its own and interpretations in conformity with its narrow interests.

In modern times, Sayyid Qutb (d. 1966) reproduces the jihadist theory in a new formula in his book *Maʿālim fī al-ṭarīq* (*Milestones*), which had a significant impact on contemporary jihadist movements:

> Since the objective of the message of Islam is a decisive declaration of man's freedom, not merely on the philosophical plane but also in the actual conditions of life, it must employ Jihad . . . Those who look for causes of a defensive nature in the history of the expansion of Islam are caught by the

> aggressive attacks of the orientalists at a time when Muslims possess neither glory nor do they possess Islam . . . Of course, in that case the defense of the "homeland of Islam" is the defense of the Islamic beliefs, the Islamic way of life, and the Islamic community. However, its defense is not the ultimate objective of the Islamic movement of Jihad but is a means of establishing the Divine authority within it so that it becomes the headquarters for the movement of Islam, which is then to be carried throughout the earth to the whole of mankind, as the object of this religion is all humanity and its sphere of action is the whole earth.[19]

In the text, we find a clear justification for aggressive warfare across the planet and against the rest of humanity, which is perennial war by nature, in the name of Islam and freedom. We also note the connection between jihād, in the war sense, and mission, *daʿwa*, which are organically correlated in his vision. He accuses those who adopt defensive warfare and reject expansionist conquests of cowardice and disbelief. It is a radical dualistic and idealistic vision that could be a messianic eschatology at best. However, when it turns into a political project, it is doomed to failure in the face of reality's complexity, regardless of the dramatic ethical implications.

It is essential to dismantle the past and modern war ideologies. The discourse of Ribʿī Ibn ʿĀmir, recycled by Sayyid Qutb,[20] is a good example, but not a unique case, of the use of history in contemporary ideologies. Qutb's thought, which inspired extremist and terrorist groups, confirms Girard's intuition that terrorism in the name of Islam "hijacks religious codes for its own purposes." Islamist terrorism "is both linked to Islam and different from it."[21] Girard affirms that this new form of violence "would not have taken such a hold on people's minds if it did not bring up to date something that has always been present in Islam."[22] This temptation has indeed been present since the beginning, but I would insist that it is not essentially or necessarily "Islamic" in the religious sense of Islam.

All-Against-One

In conclusion, a Girardian reading of Islamic historical narratives is possible. We notice a series of mimetic cycles emerging from the mechanisms of scapegoating and all-against-one. Some episodes of these narratives transcend the historical realism to embrace a mythical horizon.

Immediately before the Hegira, the Prophet Muḥammad's immigration from Mecca to Yathrib (Medina) in the year 622, the different clans of his tribe, Quraysh, who were constantly competing did agree to kill him, seeing in his mission a threat for their interests and ancestral system. To avoid reactions and a possible cycle of revenge, they chose a young man from each clan, so the "responsibility for his blood would lie upon all the clans."[23] On the night of the execution, they did not find the Prophet who had already left the city; they found in his bed his cousin, the young ʿAlī Ibn Abī Ṭālib.

In Medina, the Prophet was no longer a marginal person but the head of an emerging free community. The same mechanism occurs again: Quraysh, who saw in that community an existential threat to eliminate, formed an enlarged tribal alliance, including a well-armed Jewish tribe, Banū Qurayẓa. Medina's siege failed due to a trench, *khandaq*, which was the idea of Salmān the Persian. The Ḥudaybiya truce and then the peaceful conquest of Mecca, as we have seen, were the events that led to the community's resurrection, the end of a violent trap, and the beginning of a new era.

In these two episodes, the Prophet's life was saved. In the third episode, however, the life of his grandson was not spared. The victim was Ḥusayn, the son of ʿAlī and Fāṭima, of whom the Prophet used to say: "Ḥusayn is from me, and I am from Ḥusayn."[24] As if the two previous failures have accumulated a greater desire for revenge. They succeeded finally in killing Muḥammad in his grandson. The protagonists of the first attempts took the power, and the army of the nascent *Islamic* empire that of the Umayyads besieged the Prophet's family in Karbalāʾ in 680, half a century after Muḥammad's death, committing a terrible massacre that did not spare even newborns. Women, including the Prophet's granddaughters, were taken as prisoners of war, *sabāyā*, to the palaces of power in Kūfa and Damascus. It was a bloody foundation of the empire, which recalls Girard's idea of the "founding murder" and "the sacrificial ritual" as the origin of institution and culture.[25]

Ḥusayn's martyrdom was apparently without resurrection; but symbolically Zaynab, his sister, could be seen as the risen one, or rather "the rising sun,"[26] as she was described in the sources, facing the powerful men of her time. In the palace of Kūfa's governor, to humiliate her in front of Ḥusayn's head, ʿUbayd Allāh Ibn Ziyād asked her: "How do you judge what God has done to the people of your house?" Zaynab replied with grace and dignity: "I see nothing but beauty."[27] Resurrection is somehow the unbreakable justice of the victim that defeats the oppressor's death mentality. The same city, Kūfa, has become Najaf, which contains the Mausoleum of Ḥusayn, and testifies to the defeat of the powerful rulers.

From an eschatological perspective, al-Mahdī, the Well-Guided, called also the Risen, al-Qā᾽im, who will be of the lineage of the Prophet according to Tradition, is the resurrection of Ḥusayn. Symbolically, as if Muḥammad was killed in Ḥusayn to resurrect in Mahdī. The relationship between Ḥusayn and Mahdī is clear in the Shiʿi Tradition, as Mohammad Ali Amir-Moezzi summarizes well:

> The Qā᾽im returns to avenge the death of al-Ḥusayn. In a number of traditions, it is said that after the massacre at Karbalā᾽ the angels broke out in sobs and went to wail before God, asking Him whether He was going to let the assassination of "His Chosen One," "The Son of His Messenger," go unpunished. God replied that the revenge would take place when the Qā᾽im had his triumphal return. In other traditions, it is the angel Gabriel who informs the Prophet of the tragic fate of his grandson, adding that al-Ḥusayn will be avenged by his own ninth descendent, the Qā᾽im. According to the imams, the fact of separating ʿAlī, the only true initiate of the Prophet, from power, and rejecting his version of the Qur᾽ān, the only complete version, struck a fatal blow to Islam as a community religion for the salvation of humanity; but the real coup de grace was the assassination of al-Ḥusayn. The Muslim Community, with the exception of the small minority that remained faithful to the teachings of the imams, was thenceforth a Community composed of "enemies" of the imams and their partisans. With the assassination of a divine initiate, especially one who was the grandson and inheritor of the Prophet, "official Islam" condemned itself to flounder in violence, corruption, and oppression. This is why, in order to reestablish order and justice, one of the aspects of the final mission of the Mahdī consists in avenging al-Ḥusayn's death; in this way, majority Islam can be purged of the most despicable crime that it has ever committed.[28]

It is legitimate to ask at this point whether the martyrdom of the Imams and the People of the Prophetic House, *Ahl al-Bayt*, was a decisive step in their veneration, which in some Shiʿi circles has taken the form of divinization.[29] In Shiʿi Tradition, the murder of Ḥusayn is not the exception but the rule; the majority of the Imams were murdered. It seems that this hypothesis is plausible according to a Girardian perspective.

More or less simultaneously with the massacres committed against the Prophet's family, the scapegoat mechanism is verified on another front: the conquests, *al-futūḥāt*. They were sometimes a way to cushion internal conflicts, directing these conflicts toward external fronts on distant borders. Later, the victim is resurrected, the defeated peoples become the new leaders of the empire and in their turn other nations' conquerors. The Persians, for example, who have lost their empire, have become the vanguard of Islamic civilization; their contributions to the foundation of Islamic sciences are undeniable.

The Abbasid revolution succeeded in overthrowing the Umayyads' power, in 750 CE, because it was able to bring together all the factions that suffered from the politics of the Arab empire, in the logic of all-against-one. The Abbasids created a broad alliance that was more representative of the new plural reality, including the conquered peoples. The Arab empire died to make room for a more globalized empire. This same new empire has returned to haunt others, especially those considered as a possible threat, including those who participated in the regime change. In this context, the presumed *victims*, the Umayyads, were not innocent but rather unable to adapt themselves to the new situation and manage it adequately. The conquest prey was bigger than their mouths. The Umayyads, survivors of the Abbasid revolution, refugees and founders of a new caliphate in Andalusia, became symbols of pluralism and tolerance because they learned from experience.

This analysis is not intended to devalue the achievements of Islamic civilization and its great empires in the fields of knowledge and art, knowing that the Islamic sciences, with their methodologies and various ramifications, were born during the prosperity of Islamic civilization. The history of Islamic societies cannot be reduced to the history of empires and their conquests and defeats. It is not a mere cycle of violent mimetism. This analysis aims to deal with violence in Islamic history, adopting a critical vision that allows us to recognize the dark side of human experience in order to eventually overcome the past's knots.

Modern Challenges

Most religions are a premodern phenomenon born in a cultural context different from that of today. Western modernity has inaugurated a new world with the slogan of science and progress. The human being seemed to overcome the religious explanation of reality gradually, moving toward a phase dominated by reason with its modern knowledge, ideologies, and ideals. Modernity poses a severe challenge to religions around the world: because of globalized capitalism and colonial rule, on the one hand, and because of the epistemological revolutions at the level of the natural and physical sciences, as well as at the level of the humanities, on the other hand. It is a historical moment in which it seems that the human being would have taken his destiny in hand, to the point of no longer needing religious doctrines.

Reform movements attempt to respond to modernity's challenges to ensure their respective religions' survival in a rapidly changing world. Paradoxically, what empowered religions in this decisive historical moment is modernity itself, or, better, its current crisis, called postmodernity. Despite its triumphs, modernity suffers from a profound crisis of meaning, which has made it possible to speak of the "return of religion."

Modernity, which supports the primacy of reason and human freedom, has found itself naked in the face of the scandal of violence. Modern violence has taken unprecedented dimensions in an increasingly systematic and rationalized way, with extraordinary brutality and an unprecedented capacity to kill and exterminate.

Modernity is partially a product of extreme and systematic violence: from the invasion of the Americas to the extermination of its peoples and the plundering of their riches. The transferred gold to the treasures of European kingdoms and republics has formed the material basis of emerging capitalism; besides, the kidnapping and enslaving of millions of Africans to serve the white man's interests. Slavery is a significant example of these transformations. It was a phenomenon that preceded the rise of capitalism but took on "industrial" dimensions as a result of the "rationalization" of slave-trafficking methods, making them more "efficient" and "productive" than ever.

The turning point that opened the eyes of many people in the West and worldwide to the violent nature of modernity was World War I, then World

War II, resulted in millions of deaths and people living with physically, psychologically, and mentally disabilities. These wars awakened people from the idealistic dream of continuous progress. The Holocaust is peculiarity not only by the colossal number of victims (Jews, the Romani people, people with disabilities, gay men) but also by the rational methods and techniques in organizing the camps and killing people. There was a precise protocol; everything was done with perfect planning, in a "scientific" way, in cold blood and by "clean" hands. Science was used to kill and exterminate human beings. Indeed, it was not the first massacre in human history, but it was horribly "industrial" and "rational."

The list of modern atrocities includes also the massacres committed as a result of colonialism in the nineteenth and twentieth centuries in Africa and Asia: as the massacres committed by Belgium in Congo, about ten million people were exterminated in twenty-three years, in the second half of the nineteenth century. The Algerian War of Independence (1954–1962) killed 1.5 million Algerians, not counting previous casualties in a total of 132 years of French occupation. As for the Vietnam War, it resulted in—according to Vietnamese estimates—the deaths of one million Vietnamese soldiers and four million civilians by US forces in the 1960s and 1970s.

World War II ended in 1945, with the United States dropping two nuclear bombs on the Japanese cities of Hiroshima and Nagasaki. More than two hundred thousand people were killed, the vast majority of them civilians, including children, women, and the elderly. The two bombs wiped out all aspects of life in the two cities for decades, including animals, plants, and buildings, not to mention nuclear radiation victims. Thus, a race has begun to acquire the nuclear bomb and other weapons of mass destruction, threatening to destroy the planet and humanity several times. Modern warfare technology has evolved to make the meaning of war utterly different from what humanity has known throughout history. Modern warfare confronts us with the dilemma of avoiding civilian casualties, given the enormous extent of the destruction. Violence has characterized Western modernity and its accompanying ideologies of domination and racism. It is one of the most significant challenges that humanity must face today, with all its religions.

Listing modernity's horrors does not mean generalizing or belittling the important cultural and scientific achievements that have benefited people in various fields. The aim is to study the evolution of the violence phenomenon, which ultimately led to the emergence of a radical nonviolent religious awareness as one of the aspects of the great battle for reform.

The relationship between religions and nonviolence experienced a crucial historical shift, the "Gandhian moment," which proposed nonviolence in a new and radical way. We had to wait for the twentieth century to reach this level of consciousness. Previously, humanity had known nonviolent precursors, exemplified by the behavior of individuals and groups who favored nonviolence as a way of life. However, modernity has given the issue a systematic and political character. The "peaceful resistance," satyagraha, of Mahatma Gandhi (d. 1948), was inspired by ancient roots, such as the principle of ahimsa in Hinduism and Jainism. Nevertheless, the new dimension that this idea took on in the twentieth century was not possible without a series of circumstances, which prompted human awareness of a radical and inclusive nonviolent vision.

Perhaps the most important of these conditions—as already mentioned—is technical development, which has made war more destructive than any previous war in the premodern era. The emergence of mass destruction weapons, nuclear, hydrogen, chemical and biological bombs, and even "conventional" weapons, have become more deadly, in a way that so-called "collateral damage" cannot be avoided. In large numbers, they are often unarmed civilians. The ferocious and criminal face of war is more evident than ever. Once, chivalry values were used to justify and embellish the armed struggle, such as courage, sacrifice, generosity, solidarity with the oppressed, and justice restoration. The warrior cavalier was the one who wore these noble qualities, depicted seated on a horse, holding the sword, crossing the ranks of enemies. This heroic image of courage has become impossible today because war has become cowardly by definition. The soldier stands in front of the computer screen, enough for him to press a few buttons to cause a level of destruction that the cavalier of the past could never reach. Modern empires or "tiger democracies," in order not to lose soldiers in battle and provoke the anger of voters and public opinion, prefer to shed the blood of civilians in other countries, where the victims are politically "irrelevant."[30]

The Gandhian vision aims at a double liberation of the human being: freeing him or her from the external violence, colonialism, or tyranny, and simultaneously freeing him or her from the inner violence, so the victim will not be in the aggressor's image and likeness, reproducing the same abuses. This new vision had a significant impact on global religious thinking. On a Christian level, one cannot imagine Martin Luther King Jr. (d. 1968), Nelson Mandela (d. 2013), or Desmond Tutu (d. 2022) without the Gandhian precedent. On the Islamic level, Gandhi's influence appears first in a group of Muslims around him, who collaborated with him to liberate India and who adopted radical nonviolence, expressed and justified in an Islamic way. Among these are Abdul Ghaffar Khan (d. 1988),[31] Maulana Abul Kalam Azad (d. 1958),[32] and, after them, Asghar Ali Engineer (d. 2013).[33] Outside the Indian context, we find thinkers and activists like the Sudanese Mahmoud Mohammed Taha (d. 1985),[34] the Syrian Jawdat Said,[35] the Iranian Ramin Jahanbegloo,[36] and the American Palestinian Mohammed Abu-Nimer.[37] If we want to summarize modern Islamic thinking on nonviolence in one sentence, we find nothing better than Pope Francis's words: "Authentic Islam and the proper reading of the Qur'ān are opposed to every form of violence."[38]

The Arab Spring (2011) and the Green Wave in Iran (2009) are concrete proofs that nonviolence is no longer a marginal thought in the Islamic world. Nonviolence has become a public opinion and a popular movement, despite the tremendous obstacles and difficulties caused by the old regimes and terrorism. This is why dictatorial regimes fear nonviolent movements more since they are aware of their moral superiority, which unmasks official propaganda. When they are not overthrown by surprise as in Tunisia, oppressive regimes prefer to react with the utmost violence to provoke a violent reaction, thus attracting opposition to the field that the governments know best, namely that of battle. Everyone must be dirty and bloodstained, finally equal in evil and terror. The antithesis of war and terrorist madness, governmental or anarchist, is precisely nonviolence.

The all-against-one mechanism occurs when the people unite against the dictator to expel him. With the expulsion of the symbol of evil, it is expected that all the problems of the country will disappear. The dictator is far from being innocent, but he is undoubtedly diabolized to facilitate expulsion. Paradoxically, his departure causes great chaos, not only because the dome of fear that imposed a forced discipline has been removed, but also because there is a tiny dictator within each of us, who is the bitter fruit of a repressive culture. The political dictator is nothing more than the mirror of an oppressed and oppressive society. The all-against-one mechanism leads to the dictator's expulsion, but it does not automatically mean people's resurrection and liberation. Creating a democratic state requires the foundation of a democratic society with a democratic culture, which is a long and challenging path.

Terror in the name of Islam is competing with the new nonviolent awareness. What makes the situation more complicated is that terrorism is twisted with nationalism and populism. White supremacists use Christianity as a super clan identity, as Jewish, Hindu, and Buddhist supremacists do with their respective religions. The tango-dance between terrorism and populism creates a dangerous escalation on the international level, especially when combined with mass-destruction technology and imperial mimetic rivalry. This explosive situation, combined with the weakness of the United Nations and the failure of international law, makes relations and conflicts dominated by power and brutality. The Palestinian question is an eloquent example of this dramatic condition. Girard is aware of this global escalation, as summarized by Thomas Scheffler:

> Girard explains the rise of this "completely new configuration of violence"[39] by two different assumptions. On the one hand, he considers Islamism as "the vanguard of a general revenge against the West's wealth" and a "response to the oppression of the Third World as a whole."[40] On the other hand, he reads it "as a kind of event internal to the development of technology,"[41] "a modern effort to counter the most powerful and refined tool of the Western world: technology."[42] With his reference to technology, Girard implicitly relates the rise of Islamism to an important subject of "asymmetric warfare" theories: In wars between technologically unequal opponents, the weaker side must try to compensate for its technological inferiority by a stronger cultural and emotional mobilization of its followers. In addition, the enormous destructive power of modern arms is raising the costs and sacrifices of modern warfare to a degree that they can only be justified by extremely polarizing and emotionalizing hate and/or salvation ideologies.[43]

As Scheffler notices, Girard anticipated what other experts, like Olivier Roy, argued—that our world is not so much witnessing a "radicalization of Islam" but an "Islamization of radicalism."[44] Islamist terrorism is "something new that exploits Islamic codes, but does not at all belong to classical Islamic theory. Today's terrorism is new, even from an Islamic point of view."[45] In Girard's view, the big challenge is not only Islamic but global. For this reason, the mimetic theory is an adequate instrument to distinguish between the theology of power that leads to war and escalation and the theology of peace and nonviolence. The destiny of humanity is one, and the way of salvation is one: religions can be ways of salvation if they succeed in liberating themselves from the heavy burden of imperial nightmares.

On the intellectual and spiritual levels, radical nonviolence demands the redefinition of religion's mission in order to see it as a humanization mission, which exorcizes and disarms the human being from all forms of violence. It requires the complete abandonment of violence as the supreme goal toward which humanity moves gradually. The ethical conscience rises in history to reach peace in all its internal and external levels, its spiritual and social dimensions. The quite spontaneous and leaderless all-against-one revolutions are not enough to establish a peaceful society. The Indian Maulana Wahiduddin Khan[46] describes the all-inclusive nonviolence in this way:

> Non-violence should never be confused with inaction or passivity. Non-violence is action in the full sense of the word. Rather it is more forceful an action than that of violence. It is a fact that non-violent activism is more powerful and effective than violent activism. Non-violent activism is not limited in its sphere. It is a course of action which may be followed in all matters.[47]

Wahiduddin Khan emphasizes nonviolence's efficiency and its taking on various forms to become a lifestyle and a method of living and doing in all fields. All this requires creative thinking, which is capable of creating new forms of work and cooperation. Nonviolence requires speaking the truth to the oppressor, publicly denouncing injustice, and working hard to end the oppression. It is a very courageous and dangerous task that puts lives at risk and possibly leads to martyrdom.

Inclusive and universal peace, the project of radical nonviolence, is present in many religions, as a messianic dream postponed to the end of history and then to Paradise, as a metahistorical and eschatological hope. Today, in present history, the prevailing opinion is the theory of just or defensive war, which many religions find very difficult to overcome. Sometimes, we also find a regression to the theory of preventive and offensive warfare. The theory of permanent warfare is not yet dead. It is in the form of large or small powers that do not even recognize the minimum moral conditions of war. The debate is still open, but the awareness of nonviolence as a fundamental solution to the tragedies of war, killings, and displacements has begun to crystallize and present itself as an alternative and a new horizon.

Notes

Introduction. Interpreting Girard's Silence

1. James G. Williams (tr.), Orbis Books, Maryknoll, New York, 2001. All references to this book are indicated by the abbreviation "RG," followed by the page number.
2. According to Girard, Christianity is unique because it is in continuity and discontinuity with early religions; this paradoxical relationship enabled Christianity to be "transformative" toward the pagan heritage. Girard later attenuated his initial radical approach to the opposition between archaic sacrifice and Christ's sacrifice: "the use of the same word for both types of sacrifice, as misleading as it may be on one level, nevertheless suggests something essential, namely, the paradoxical unity of religion in all its forms throughout human history." Girard, *The One by Whom Scandal Comes*, M. B. DeBevoise (tr.), Michigan State University Press, East Lansing, 2014, p. 43. See also: Wolfgang Palaver, *Transforming the Sacred into Saintliness: Reflecting on Violence and Religion with René Girard*, Cambridge University Press, Cambridge, 2020, pp. 68–69.
3. Jn 7, 53–8, 11.
4. RG 85.
5. "Islam and Islamism in the Mirror of Girard's Mimetic Theory," in *Mimetic Theory and Islam: "The Wound Where Light Enters,"* M. Kirwan and A. Achtar (eds.), Palgrave Macmillan, New York, 2019, p. 129. See: G. De Tanoüarn and L. Lineul, "Entretien avec René Girard," *La nouvelle revue Certitudes* 16, 2003, p. 42.
6. Girard, *Battling to the End: Conversations with Benoît Chantre*, Mary Baker (tr.), Michigan State University Press, East Lansing, 2010, p. 214.
7. Jacques Dupuis, *Toward a Christian Theology of Religious Pluralism*, Orbis Books, New York, 1997.
8. "Mimetic Theory and Islam," Heythrop College of London University, November 5–7, 2013.
9. "Mimetic Theory and Islam," School of Catholic Theology at the University of Innsbruck, May 19–21, 2016.

Chapter One. Theory and Principles

1. RG 88.

2. Ismāʿīl Rājī al-Fārūqī (d. 1986) is an American-Palestinian Muslim philosopher, theologian, and expert in comparative religions. He elaborated the concept of "the Islamization of knowledge" and cofounded the International Institute for Islamic Thought (IIIT) in Virginia (USA) in order to develop this idea. See: Abdulhamid Abusulayman, *Islamization of Knowledge: General Principles and Work Plan*, IIIT, 1988; and Imtiyaz Yusuf (ed.), *Islam and Knowledge: Al Faruqi's Concept of Religion in Islamic Thought*, I. B. Tauris, London, 2012. This approach is largely debated and criticized among Muslims. See: Seyyed Vali Reza Nasr, "Islamization of Knowledge: A Critical Overview," *Islamic Studies* 30, no. 3 (1991), pp. 387–400.

3. Girard referred, in a footnote, RG 118, to the works of François Lagarde, *René Girard ou la Christianisation des Sciences Humaines*, Peter Lang, New York, 1994; and Lucien Scubla, *Lire Lévi-Strauss*, Odile Jacob, Paris, 1998. For the Catholic approach, see: Pope John Paul II's Encyclical Letter, *Fides et Ratio*, http://w2.vatican.va/content/john-paul-ii/en/encyclicals/documents/hf_jp-ii_enc_14091998_fides-et-ratio.html.

4. René Guenon (d. 1951), known as Shaykh ʿAbd al-Wāḥid Yaḥyā, a French philosopher, among the founders of the Traditionalist school. See: *The Crisis of the Modern World*, M. Pallis, R. C. Nicholson (tr.), Sophia Perennis; Revised Edition, 2004 (1st ed. 1927); and *The Reign of Quantity and the Signs of the Times*, Sophia Perennis, 4th ed. 2004 (1st ed. 1945).

5. Seyyed Hossein Nasr is an Iranian Sufi philosopher. See his criticism of Modern humanities in: Seyyed Hossein Nasr with Ramin Jahanbegloo, *In Search of the Sacred: A Conversation with Seyyed Hossein Nasr on His Life and Thought*, Praeger, Santa Barbara, CA, 2010, pp. 171–234.

6. Malek Bennabi (d. 1973) is an Algerian thinker and reformist. In his book, *Les Conditions de la Renaissance*, Editions ANEP, Alger, 1ère ed. 1948, 2005, pp. 49, 67–80, he developed what he called the equation of civilization: Man + Soil + Time = Civilization, and of which religion forms the catalyst.

7. RG 88–89, 93–94.

8. In other works, Girard used more moderate tones, confirming that even those "religions of violence" were "always in search of peace." See: *Things Hidden since the Foundation of the World*, in collaboration with Jean-Michel Oughourlian and Guy Lefort, S. Bann and M. Metteer (tr.), Stanford University Press, Stanford, 1987, p. 401.

9. RG 89.

10. RG 90.

11. In Girard's last book, he criticized himself for being too idealistic in his earlier work. See: Girard, *Battling to the End*, pp. 106–108.

12. Qur'ānic quotations are taken from several translations. The website www.tanzil.net helped me compare eighteen translations and choose the one best suited to the context. I used especially Talal Itani's translation, sometimes making modifications if necessary. I used also M. A. S. Abdel Haleem (Oxford University Press, Oxford, 2004), which is not included on the website. The first number in parentheses indicates the number of the sūra, and the second one indicates the number of the verse.
13. Muhammad Iqbal is an Indian philosopher and reformist, and is considered the founder of the idea of Pakistan. See: Iqbal, *The Reconstruction of Religious Thought in Islam*, M. Saeed Sheikh (ed.), Stanford University Press, Iqbal Academy Pakistan, Stanford, 2013, pp. 100–101.
14. RG 93.
15. RG 91.
16. RG 105.
17. Victims' divinization in pagan mythology has nothing to do with Jesus's Resurrection, as Girard emphasizes: "If Jesus's death were sacrificial, the Resurrection would be the 'product' of the Crucifixion. But this is not so. Orthodox theology has always successfully resisted the temptation to transform the Passion into a process that endows Jesus with divinity. In orthodox terms, Christ's divinity—though it is obviously not external to his humanity—is not dependent on the events of his earthly life. Instead of making the Crucifixion a cause of his divinity—which is a constant temptation for Christians—it is preferable to see it as a consequence of the latter." *Things Hidden*, p. 233. See also: RG 132, and especially RG 133–136.
18. RG 108–109.
19. RG 110.
20. RG 109–110.
21. RG 104.
22. RG 106–107.
23. RG 107.
24. RG 108.
25. The first Muslims were aware of this similarity. In a ḥadīth: "When the Prophet arrived in Medina, he found the Jews observing the fast of 'Āshūrā' [10th of Muḥarram]. He asked: 'What is this?' Whereupon they said: 'This is the day on which Moses and the Israelites were granted victory over Pharaoh, therefore we fast on that day in order to glorify it.' Then the Prophet said: 'We are even more closely associated with Moses than you,' and he ordered his followers to fast on that day too." G. H. A. Juynboll, *Encyclopedia of Canonical Ḥadīth*, Brill, Leiden, 2007, p. 517.
26. Ex 20, 2–17.

27. M. A. Draz, *Introduction to the Qur'ān*, I. B. Tauris, London, 2000, pp. 66–67.
28. RG 11–12.
29. Juynboll, *Encyclopedia of Canonical Ḥadīth*, p. 676. The translation is modified.
30. RG 33.
31. RG 40.
32. RG 42.
33. RG 87.
34. Al-Nawawī, *Riyāḍ al-Ṣāliḥīn: A Translation and Commentary*, Moulana Afzal Ismail (ed.), Muslims at Work Publications, Heidelberg (South Africa), 2nd ed. 2016, ḥadīths 1809, 1817, 1818, vol. 3, pp. 439, 444. The translation is modified.
35. RG 44–45.
36. RG 42.
37. Mālik b. Anas, *al-Muwaṭṭa'*, M. Fadel and Monette (tr.), Harvard University Press, Cambridge, MA, 2019, ḥadīth 547, p. 198. God will not accept their recitation of the Qur'ān, or their recitation is only a vocal without any understanding. Despite this group's excessive performance of ritual devotions, recitation of the Qur'ān, performance of prayers, and fasting, they fail to internalize any of the essential meanings of Islam.
38. Acts (4, 26), which mirrors Psalm (2, 2). RG 95.
39. RG 96.
40. RG 93.
41. The *Basmala* is mentioned at the beginning of every sūra, except sūra 9 (*al-Tawba*). However, it is mentioned twice in sūra 27 (*al-Naml*), in the beginning, then in verse 30.
42. Ibn 'Arabī philosophically developed the relationship between Mercy and creation. See: Toshihiko Izutsu, *Sufism and Taoism: A Comparative Study of Key Philosophical Concepts*, University of California Press, Berkeley, 1983, pp. 116–140.
43. RG 14.
44. RG 15.
45. Rūmī, *Dīvān-e Shams, Ghazaliyyāt*, Ghazal (ode) 207, https://ganjoor.net/moulavi/shams/ghazalsh/sh207/, accessed April 6, 2021.
46. In this context, the Sufis use the famous ḥadīth "I was a hidden Treasure, then I desired (loved) to be known, so I created the creation in order to be known," which is considered as a comment on the mentioned verse. This ḥadīth is judged forged by the traditionists.
47. Michel Chodkiewicz, *An Ocean Without Shore: Ibn 'Arabi, the Book, and the Law*,

State University of New York Press, Albany, 1993, p. xx.

48. The word translated as "oaths" is *aymān*, plural of *yamīn*, which also means "the right hand" or "direction." This word is from the same root of *īmān*, which means "faith" or "belief." Faith is seen as a solemn oath and commitment toward God.

49. RG 9.

50. RG 11.

51. RG 122.

52. Lk 22, 53. RG 37.

53. See the detailed study of: Todd Lawson, *The Crucifixion and the Qur'ān: A Study in the History of Muslim Thought*, Oneworld Publications, Oxford, 2009. Rāzī (m. 604/1210), in his monumental commentary, mentioned ten alternative stories to the Crucifixion, then he concluded: "all these opinions are in conflict and contradiction, and God knows better!" *Tafsīr al-Rāzī, al-Tafsīr al-kabīr aw Mafātīḥ al-ghayb*, Dār al-Fikr, Beirut, 1981, vol. 11, p. 102.

54. The theory of substitution claims that God has cast the likeness of Jesus upon Judas Iscariot, who was arrested and crucified in the place of his Master, as punishment for his betrayal. It is an unacceptable theory for Ibn Ḥazm, because it attributes deception to God. See: Adnane Mokrani, *Naqd al-adyān ʿinda Ibn Ḥazm al-andalusī*, IIIT, Virginia, 2008, pp. 106–109.

55. As Mahmoud Ayoub, *A Muslim View of Christianity: Essays on Dialogue*, Irfan A. Omar (ed.), Orbis Books, New York, 2007, pp. 156–183. Other comprehensive Muslim approaches include: Mustafa Akyol, *The Islamic Jesus: How the King of the Jews Became a Prophet of the Muslims*, St Martin's Press, New York, 2017; and Navid Kermani, *Incroyable christianisme*, R. Kremer (tr.), Salvator, Paris, 2016.

56. This ḥadīth is considered by the traditionists as a forged ḥadīth. Yet it is frequently found in Sufi texts as a synthesis of the path. Javad Nurbakhsh, *Traditions of the Prophet*, Khaniqahi Nimatullahi Publications, New York, 1981, vol. 1, p. 66.

57. It is the last sentence of a popular prayer commonly attributed to St. Francis (d. 1226), which begins with: "Lord, make me an instrument of your peace." It is the same meaning of Jesus's saying: "Anyone who wants to save his life will lose it; but anyone who loses his life for my sake will find it" (Mt 16, 25), and Paul's saying: "You have died, and now the life you have is hidden with Christ in God" (Col 3, 3).

58. *Tafsīr al-Sulamī aw Ḥaqā'q al-tafsīr, tafsīr al-Qur'ān al-ʿazīz*, Sayyid ʿImrān (ed.), Dār al-kutub al-ʿilmiyya, Beirut, 2nd ed. 2016, vol. 1, p. 59. This verse has been interpreted very violently by some commentators, reading it as "kill yourselves," in the sense of killing the guilty ones or even in form of civil war and massacres. See: al-Ṭabarī, *Tafsīr al-Ṭabarī, Jāmiʿ al-bayān ʿan taʾwīl āy al-Qurʾān*, ʿAbd Allāh bin ʿAbd al-Muḥsin al-Turkī (ed.), Hajr lil-ṭibāʿa wa al-nashr, al-Jīza, Cairo, 2001, vol. 1, pp. 679–685.

59. Col 2, 14–15. RG 181.

60. For the Islamic theology of liberation, see: Asghar Ali Engineer, *Islam and Liberation Theology: Essays on Liberative Elements in Islam*, Sterling Publishers, New Delhi, 1990; and Farid Esack, *Qur'ān Liberation & Pluralism: An Islamic Perspective of Interreligious Solidarity against Oppression*, Oneworld, Oxford, 1997.

61. *L'Autre que nous attendons, homélies de père Christian de Chergé, 1970–1996*, Editions de Bellefontaine, 2006. An Italian extract is published on the Vatican website, accessed March 25, 2019, https://w2.vatican.va/content/osservatore-romano/it/comments/2010/documents/299q01b1.html.

62. RG 135.

63. RG 13.

64. RG 13–14.

65. RG 14.

66. RG 15.

67. For an accurate discussion of the question of apostasy in Islam, see: Taha Jabir Alalwani, *Apostasy in Islam: A Historical and Scriptural Analysis*, N. Roberts (tr.), The International Institute of Islamic Thought (IIIT), London, 2011.

68. Jawdat Said, *Lā ikrāh fī al-dīn, dirāsāt wa abḥāth fī al-fikr al-islāmī [No Compulsion in Religion, Studies in Islamic Thought]*, M. Nafīsa (ed.), Al-ʿilm wa al-salām lil-dirāsāt wa al-nashr, Damascus, 1997, p. 27.

69. Al-Nawawī, *Riyāḍ al-Ṣāliḥīn*, ḥadīth 639, vol. 2, p. 42. The translation is modified.

70. Juynboll, *Encyclopedia of Canonical Ḥadīth*, p. 360.

71. Al-Nawawī, *Riyāḍ al-Ṣāliḥīn*, ḥadīths 309, 314, 1511, vol. 1, pp. 374, 379; vol. 3, p. 204. The translation is modified.

72. Abū Dāwūd, *Sunan Abū Dāwūd*, Sayyid Muḥammad Sayyid and others (eds.), Dār al-Ḥadīth, Cairo, 2010, ḥadīth 4800, vol. 4, p. 2051.

73. On the juridical debate about blasphemy, see: Lutz Wiederhold, "Shatm," *Encyclopaedia of Islam, Second Edition*, first published online 2012, accessed April 6, 2021, https://referenceworks.brillonline.com/browse/encyclopaedia-of-islam-2.

74. In this verse there is a reference to capital punishment, which shows that values are always inserted in their historical context. The verse most probably quotes the Mishna, Sanhedrin 4: 5. See: Amir-Moezzi, Dye (eds.), *Le Coran des Historiens*, Cerf, Paris, 2019, vol. 2a, pp. 216–217.

75. The use of the adjective "Islamic" to describe states is a modern phenomenon. Historically, Muslims used mainly dynasties' names, though the caliphate was the main instrument for religious self-legitimation. "Caliph" means the Prophet's "successor" as the community's supreme leader on the political level. Some caliphs pretended to have religious authority, despite the dogma of the end of prophethood. The modern Azhari scholar Ali Abdel Razek (d. 1966) dismantled the idea that

the caliphate is an Islamic necessity or obligation. His book was published in 1925, immediately after the abolition of the Ottoman caliphate: *Islam and the Foundations of Political Power*, M. Loutfi (tr.), A. Filali-Ansary (ed.), Edinburgh University Press, The Aga Khan University, Edinburgh, 2012. For Shiʿism, the Imams are infallible and inspired, though they rarely governed. The Guardianship of the Jurist, *Velāyat-e Faqīh*, Ayatollah Khomeini's political theory, reopened the modern Shiʿi debate in new terms. See: Constance Arminjon Hachem, *Chiisme et état: Les clercs à l'épreuve de la modernité*, CNRS Éditions, Paris, 2013.

Chapter Two. The Qurʾānic Narratives

1. Exactly 1,453 of 6,235 verses. See: Claude Gilliot, "Narratives," in *Encyclopaedia of the Qurʾān*, Jane Dammen McAuliffe (ed.), Brill, Leiden, 2003, vol. 3, p. 517.

2. See: (2, 27, 205); (5, 32–33, 64); (8, 73); (11, 116); (13, 25); (16, 88); (26, 152); (27, 48); (28, 77, 83); (30, 41); (40, 26); (89, 12).

3. Al-Ḥusayn Ibn Manṣūr al-Hallāj (d. 922), in his book *Ṭawāsīn*, said: "He [Iblīs] was asked: Prostrate [to Adam]! He said: 'Not before another than You.'" The translation is mine. *Il Cristo dell'Islam, scritti mistici*, A. Ventura (tr.), Mondadori, Milan, 2007, p. 127. Similar compassionate stories with Iblīs are found in al-Ghazālī (d. 1111), Rūzbihān Baqlī (d. 1209), and ʿAṭṭār (d. 1221), Rūmī (d. 1273). See: Stéphane Ruspoli, *Le traité de l'Esprit saint de Rûzbehân de Shîrâz*, Cerf, Paris, 2001, pp. 112–114.

4. See these two ḥadīths: "Whoever introduces a good practice, *sunna ḥasana*, that is followed after him, will have a reward for that and the equivalent of their reward, without that detracting from their reward in the slightest. Whoever introduces an evil practice, *sunna sayyiʾa*, that is followed after him, will bear the burden of sin for that and the equivalent of their burden of sin, without that detracting from their burden in the slightest." Ibn Māja, *Sunan Ibn Māja*, Book 1, ḥadīth 207, ʿAbd al-Bāqī and al-Dhahabī (eds.), Dār al-Ḥadīth, Cairo, 2010, vol. 1, p. 118. "God does not obliterate an evil deed by an evil one, but He obliterates an evil deed by a good one. What is impure does not obliterate what is impure." Al-Khaṭīb al-Tabrīzī, *Mishkāt al-Maṣābīḥ*, al-Albani (ed.), al-Maktab al-Islāmī, Beirut, 2nd ed. 1979, Book 11, ḥadīth 2771, p. 845.

5. It seems that a similar practice was present in Arabia: the Prophet's grandfather, ʿAbd al-Muṭṭalib, had to sacrifice his youngest son, ʿAbd Allāh, the future father of Muḥammad, because he made a vow that if he has ten children, he will sacrifice one of them. The son was saved through a ransom of one hundred camels. See: Ibn Isḥāq, *The Life of Muḥammad: A Translation of Ibn Isḥāq's Sīrat Rasūl Allāh*, A. Guillaume (tr.), Oxford University Press, Karachi, 1982, p. 66–68.

6. Al-Qushayrī, *Tafsīr al-Qushayrī al-musammā Laṭāʾif al-ishārāt*, ʿAbd al-Laṭīf Ḥasan ʿAbd al-Raḥmān (ed.), Dār al-kutub al-ʿilmiyya, Beirut, 3rd ed. 2015, vol. 3, p. 93.

7. Al-Sulamī, *Tafsīr al-Sulamī*, vol. 2, p. 179.

8. Al-Nawawī, *Riyāḍ al-Ṣāliḥīn*, ḥadīth 1867, vol. 3, pp. 480–481, The translation is modified.

9. It seems that in some stories the Bible emphasizes the human factor. The Qur᾿ān, on the other hand, underlines the divine Will that moves everything. Paolo Dall'Oglio offers a key to reconcile the two levels of reading in the example of Adam's story: "In the Qur᾿ān, God reveals the name of created things to Adam [2, 31], while in the Bible God is curious to know how Adam will call creatures [Gen 2, 19]. It is possible to contrast these two visions and make a theory about the free biblical man and the Qur᾿ānic man to whom the names are dictated. But this is precisely the method that disgusts me most: to compare to judge! In my opinion, it is magnificent to see how this Qur᾿ānic concept, exactly on the same line as the biblical concept, offers a meditation on rational human activity, originally seen as a revealed thought. Man united with God, God thinks in him, and human thought becomes revelation." The translation is mine. *Innamorato dell'Islam, credente in Gesù, dell'islamofilia*, Jaca Book, Milan, 2nd ed. 2013, pp. 31–32. For a detailed comparative study of Abraham's sacrifice, see: Sandor Goodhart, "Fathers and Sons, Sacrifice and Substitution: Mimetic Theory and Islam in Genesis 22 and Sura 37," *Mimetic Theory and Islam*, pp. 65–85.

10. Muslim, *Ṣaḥīḥ Muslim, English Translation*, Nasiruddin al-Khattab (tr.), Huda Khattab (ed.), Darussalam, Riyadh, 2007, vol. 3, ḥadīth 3155, p. 444. See also: ḥadīths 3152, 3153, and 3154.

11. Mālik b. Anas, *al-Muwaṭṭa᾿*, ḥadīth 1369, p. 381.

12. Michel Cuypers, *The Composition of the Qur᾿ān: Rhetorical Analysis*, Bloomsbury, London, 2016, p. 82.

13. For the interpretative debate about homosexuality in the Qur᾿ān, see: Scott Siraj al-Haqq Kugle, *Homosexuality in Islam: Critical Reflection on Gay, Lesbian, and Transgender Muslims*, Oneworld, Oxford, 2010, pp. 49–72.

14. In a conference at the Pontifical Institute for Arabic and Islamic Studies (PISAI) in Rome, January 27, 2017. Farid Esack incorporated my reflections in his article "Lot and His Offer: 2016 IQSA Presidential Address," *Journal of International Qur᾿ānic Studies Association JIQSA* 2 (2017), pp. 26–28.

15. See, for instance: Al-Ṭabarī, *Jāmiʿ al-bayān ʿan taʾwīl āy al-Qurʾān (tafsīr al-Ṭabarī)*, vol. 12, pp. 502–505. A summary of the Islamic interpretative debate can be found in: Esack, "Lot and His Offer," pp. 22–26. See also: Waleed Ahmed, "Lot's Daughters in the Qur᾿ān: An Investigation Through the Lens of Intertextuality," in *New Perspectives on the Qur᾿ān: The Qur᾿ān in Its Historical Context 2*, Gabriel S. Reynolds (ed.), Routledge, Abingdon, 2011, pp. 411–424.

16. The opinion that he intended his own daughters is attributed to ʿAbd Allāh b. ʿAbbās, Muqātil b. Sulaymān, Abū Muḥammad Sahl b. ʿAbd Allāh al-Tustarī (d. 203/818), and Abū᾿l-Ḥasan ʿAlī b. Muḥammad al-Māwardī (d. 450/1058). Esack, "Lot and His Offer," p. 24.

17. Gen 12, 11–13. This detail is absent in the Qur'ān, but it does exist in the Tradition.

18. Al-Bayhaqī, *al-Sunan al-Kubrā*, ḥadīth 16896, I. M. ʿAbd al-Ḥamīd (ed.), Dār al-Ḥadīth, Cairo, 2008, vol. 8, p. 487.

19. It was narrated from Jābir b. ʿAbd Allāh that a man said, "O Messenger of God, I have wealth and a son, and my father wants to take all my wealth." He said, "You and your wealth belong to your father." *Sunan Ibn Māja*, ḥadīths 2291–2292, vol. 2, p. 315. The ḥadīth can be understood as a call for family sodality and taking care of the parents. Unfortunately, this text could be used to justify parental violence against children. In some juridical schools, the father cannot be punished for killing his son or daughter.

20. In classical Islamic law, the father cannot oblige his daughter to marry whom she has refused, but her silence can be interpreted as acceptance.

21. Al-Qurṭubī attributes this opinion to Abū ʿUbayda Maʿmar b. al-Muthannā (d. 207/822), Abū ʿAbd Allāh ʿIkrima b. ʿAbd Allāh (d. 105/723), and others. *Tafsīr al-Qurṭubī*, S. M. al-Badrī (ed.), Dār al-kutub al-ʿilmiyya, Beirut, 4th ed. 2014, vol. 5, p. 51.

22. See a detailed analysis of the story in: Paolo Dall'Oglio, *Speranza nell'Islam, Interpretazione della prospettiva escatologica di Corano XVIII*, Marietti, Genova, 1991, pp. 241–291.

23. Bilqīs, and sometimes Balqīs, is the name of the Queen of Sheba in the Islamic exegetical literature, never mentioned in the Qur'ān by name. The only woman named in the Qur'ān is Mary, the mother of Jesus Christ.

24. See: Jacob Lassner, *Demonizing the Queen of Sheba: Boundaries of Gender and Culture in Postbiblical Judaism and Medieval Islam*, University of Chicago Press, Chicago, 1993.

25. The worship of the sun represents an intermediate stage between polytheism and transcendental monotheism. See the story of Abraham in the Qur'ān (6, 74–81).

26. The Qur'ān does not attribute to Solomon the worship of foreign gods and building temples for them (1 Kings 11, 1–8). We find, instead, a sign of a softer weakness: "When We decreed Solomon's death, nothing showed the jinn he was dead, but a [little] worm of the earth eating away his stick: when he fell down they realized if they had known what was hidden they would not have continued their demeaning labor" (34, 14). The body of Solomon fell to the ground because "a [little] worm of the earth." The unbeatable king so feared by the jinn fell too. When the king died, who used to laugh watching the ants, his body fell because of an insect. The same image shows the signs of weakness of his subjects, who were able to bring the throne of Sheba in the blink of an eye. His relative imperfection is manifested in other episodes (38, 31–42). Solomon and Job in the Qur'ān form a couple of parables of extreme power and extreme weakness—parables of thanksgiving for the first, and patience for the second.

27. The letter is described in Arabic as *karīm*, which is translated as "noble" or

"gracious." Here I prefer the translation by Yusuf Ali that means "worthy of respect," or "a truly distinguished letter," which are more accurate translations for the threat included in the letter.

28. The word *insān*, meaning "a human being," is neutral, indicating the man and the woman.

29. In English, the distinction between the two thrones is with the articles "a/the," and with the use of lowercase/uppercase. In the original text, however, the difference is expressed by the absence or presence of the definite article *al*, the presence of which indicates the uniqueness and comprehensiveness: *ʿarsh ʿaẓīm / al-ʿarsh al-ʿaẓīm*. Throughout the Qurʾān, the word *ʿarsh*, throne, is attributed only to God and the Queen of Sheba.

30. See the interpretation of Rūmī in: *The Mathnawi*, Book IV, verses 862–888, R. A. Nicholson (tr.), Cambridge University Press, London, 1930, pp. 319–321.

31. Sacred art, for Souad Ayada, is an instrument of conversion and reception of prophecy gifts: "Art is a human activity that creates objects that are not appearances or illusions; they are rather real appearances and true illusions. As such, it is part of the prophetic activity. The *ṣarḥ* [the hall or the palace] visited by Bilqīs is an artifice that errs and saves the Queen of Sheba, actualizing a faculty possessed by God's elected people: the prophetic imagination. This faculty does not overlap with the common use of the imagination that men do. It is a visionary faculty that gives a form of appearance to invisible beings. The prophetic imagination does not abstract the intelligible from the sensible to make them knowable. It proceeds in a reverse movement by concretizing the supersensible realities to make them visible. These supersensible realities are not fictions; they belong to the divine world." *L'islam des théophanies, une religion à l'épreuve de l'art*, CNRS Éditions, Paris, 2010, p. 51. The translation is mine. To deepen the aesthetic interpretation, see: Valérie Gonzales, *Le Piège de Salomon: La Pensée de l'art dans le Coran*, Albin Michel, Paris, 2002. *Beauty and Islam: Aesthetics in Islamic Art and Architecture*, The Institute of Ismaili Studies, I. B. Tauris, London, 2001, especially the chapter "The Aesthetics of the Solomonic Parable in the Qurʾān," pp. 26–41.

Chapter Three. The Historical Narratives

1. Al-Bukhārī, *al-Tārīkh al-Kabīr*, Dāʾirat al-maʿārif al-ʿuthmāniyya, Hyderabad Deccan, vol. 2, p. 81. This ḥadīth is considered weak according to traditional criteria. See: Al-Albānī, *Silsilat al-aḥādīth al-ḍaʿīfa wa al-mawḍūʿa*, Maktabat al-maʿārif, Riyad, 1992, vol. 2, pp. 268–269.

2. Ibn Māja, *Sunan Ibn Māja*, ḥadīth 2779, vol. 2, p. 502. This ḥadīth is considered weak. Daylam is the name of a mountainous region of inland Gilan in the current Iran. These ḥadīths speak of Constantinople's conquest as an eschatological sign. Some talk of peaceful and symbolic conquest when the city's walls fall because of the prayers.

3. Al-Suyūṭī (d. 1505) mentioned a saying attributed to Aḥmad Ibn Ḥanbal (d. 855): "Three (genre of books) are baseless, *tafsīr*, the Qur'ānic commentary, *malāḥim*, the eschatological battles, and *maghāzī*, the military expeditions. This is because most of them contain traditions from the following (*marāsīl*)." *Marāsīl*, pl. of *mursal*, ḥadīth reported simply, without naming the Companions of the Prophet who would have heard them, which is considered as a defect. *Le parfait manuel des sciences coraniques al-Itqān fī 'ulūm al-Qur'ān*, Michel Lagarde (tr.), Brill, Leiden, 2018, vol. 2, p. 1261.

4. In the bibliographical work of Ibn al-Nadīm (d. 990), there are many books that contain the term *maghāzī* in their titles. See: *al-Fihrist*, Reza Tajaddod (ed.), printed by the editor, Tehran, 1971, pp. 105, 106, 114, 117, 122, 147, 252, 282, 284, 287. Among the oldest books of this genre is: Ma'mar Ibn Rāshid (d. 770), *The Expeditions: An Early Biography of Muḥammad, According to the Recension of 'Abd al-Razzāq al-Ṣan'ānī*, Sean W. Anthony (tr.), New York University Press, New York, 2015.

5. On the origin and development of the jihadist theory, see: Asma Afsaruddin, *Striving in the Path of God: Jihād and Martyrdom in Islamic Thought*, Oxford University Press, New York, 2013; and Kenneth A. Goudie, *Reinventing Jihād: Jihād Ideology from the Conquest of Jerusalem to the End of the Ayyūbids (c. 492/1099–647/1249)*, Brill, Leiden, 2019.

6. Ibn Isḥāq, *The Life of Muḥammad*, p. 500. The reason for Quraysh refusal was to avoid any contact between the Prophet and the Arabs, especially in the time of pilgrimage, which was and still is the most significant gathering.

7. Ibn Isḥāq, *The Life of Muḥammad*, p. 507. The truce was intended for ten years, but it was broken by a group allied with Quraysh two years later.

8. Ibn Isḥāq, *The Life of Muḥammad*, pp. 505–506. See also: Al-Ṭabarī, *Jāmi' al-bayān*, vol. 21, p. 238.

9. Ibn Isḥāq, *The Life of Muḥammad*, pp. 552–553.

10. In 2014, the Criminal Court in the Mauritanian city of Nouadhibou sentenced Mohamed Cheikh Ould Mkhaitir to death, due to the publication of an article in which he mentioned this contradiction—in his opinion—between the Prophet's treatment of Banū Qurayẓa and his pardon for the Quraysh after the conquest of Mecca. He was released after the appeal in 2017. The case background is related to former slaves and discrimination against them in Mauritania.

11. See: Michael Lecker, *The "Constitution of Medina": Muḥammad's First Legal Document*, The Darwin Press, Princeton, 2004.

12. See: Ibn Isḥāq, *The Life of Muḥammad*, pp. 461–469. See the debate about the authenticity of the sources and the contradictory numbers of men sentenced to death: Sadik Kirazli, "Re-Examining the Story of the Banū Qurayẓah Jews in Medina with Reference to the Account of Ibn Isḥāq," *Australian Journal of Islamic Studies* 4, no. 1 (2019), pp. 1–17. Rizwi S. Faizer, "Muḥammad and the Medinan Jews: A Comparison of the Texts of Ibn Isḥāq's Kitāb Sīrat Rasūl Allāh with

al-Wāqidī's Kitāb al-Maghāzī," *International Journal of Middle East Studies*, 28, 1996, pp. 463–489. Walid Arafat, "New Light on the Story of Banū Qurayẓa and the Jews of Medina," *Journal of the Royal Asiatic Society of Great Britain and Ireland* (1976), pp. 100–107.

13. Khālid Ibn al-Walīd got this title because he withdrew safely from the battle of Mu'ta and avoided a disaster. See: Martin Lings, *Muḥammad: His Life Based on the Earliest Sources*, Inner Traditions, VT, 2006, p. 299.

14. Ibn al-Ḥakam, *Futūḥ ifrīqiyya wa al-andalus*, A. al-Ṭabbā' (ed.), Dār al-kitāb al-lubnānī, Beirut, 1964, p. 33. There is a pun that disappears in the translation between *ifrīqiyya*, which means "Africa," or, more precisely, a zone in the current Tunisia that later gave its name to all the continent, and *mufarriqa*, from the same root *f.r.q.*, which means "dispersive."

15. See: Ibn Kathīr, *al-Bidāya wa al-nihāya*, Maktabat al-ma'ārif, Beirut, 1991, vol. 4, p. 269.

16. "Management of Savagery, the Most Critical Stage Through Which the Islamic Community Will Pass," *idārat al-tawaḥḥush, akhṭar marḥala satamur bihā al-umma*, also translated as "Administration of Savagery," is a book by Abu Bakr Naji, most probably a pseudonym, published on the internet in 2004. It aimed to provide a strategy for al-Qaeda and other extremist groups.

17. Al-Ṭabarī, *The History of al-Ṭabarī, vol. XII, the Battle of al-Qādisiyya and the Conquest of Syria and Palestine*, Yohanan Friedmann (tr.), State University of New York Press, Albany, 1992, pp. 67–68. We find later, on p. 69, the same options on the tongue of Hudhayfa Ibn Mihsan: "He [God] ordered us to summon the people to one of three options. Whichever you accept will be accepted by us. [If you embrace] Islam, we shall leave you alone. If [you agree to pay] the poll tax, we shall protect you if you need our protection. Otherwise, it is war."

18. See: J. Schacht, "Abū Ḥanīfa al-Nu'mān"; "al-Awzā'ī;" "Mālik b. Anas;" H. Laoust, "Aḥmad b. Ḥanbal," *Encyclopaedia of Islam, Second Edition*, accessed March 4, 2021, https://referenceworks.brillonline.com/browse/encyclopaedia-of-islam-2.

19. *Milestones*, Maktabah Booksellers and Publishers, Birmingham, 2006, pp. 72, 78–79, 82–83. Qutb considers the discourses of Rib'ī Ibn 'Āmir and Hudhayfa Ibn Mihsan as representative of the original Islamic position. See: *Milestones*, pp. 81, 148, 160.

20. Qutb mentioned Rib'ī Ibn 'Āmir several times. See: *Milestones*, pp. 81, 148, 160.

21. Girard, *Battling to the End*, p. 215.

22. Girard, *Battling to the End*, p. 213. See: Thomas Scheffler, "Islam and Islamism in the Mirror of Girard's Mimetic Theory," p. 132. Girard's statement that the violent elements have "always been present in Islam" does not mean, in my opinion, that these elements are *essential* to Islam.

23. Ibn Isḥāq, *The Life of Muḥammad*, p. 222.

24. Al-Tirmidhī, *Sunan al-Tirmidhī*, Ḥadīth 3775, M. M. H. al-Dhahabī (ed.), Dār

al-Ḥadīth, Cairo, 2010, vol. 5, p. 475.

25. GR, 87–94.

26. Christopher Paul Clohessy, *Half of My Heart: the Narratives of Zaynab, Daughter of ʿAlî*, Gorgias Press, Piscataway, 2018, pp. 133–137.

27. Clohessy, *Half of My Heart*, p. 179.

28. Mohammad Ali Amir-Moezzi, *The Divine Guide in Early Shiʿism: The Sources of Esotericism in Islam*, D. Streight (tr.), State University of New York Press, Albany, 1994, pp. 118–119. Majoritarian Islam, Sunnism, cannot be identified with the murders of Ḥusayn. Muslims widely condemn his assassination, and the love of the Prophet's family is well-rooted in Sunni Tradition. However, some Sunni scholars tried to defend the Umayyads or to attenuate the momentousness of Karbalāʾ. Today, Salafism represents the extremist anti-Shiʿi component of Sunnism. Simultaneously, some Shiʿi groups still consider Sunnis to be the followers of Yazīd, the Umayyad caliph who ordered the murder of Ḥusayn. See: Adnane Mokrani, "ʿĀshūrāʾ in Sunnite Mirrors: Confused Borders between Joy and Sadness," *Islamochristiana* 36 (2010), pp. 47–62.

29. See the divine attributes and features of the Imams in Amir-Moezzi, *The Divine Guide in Early Shiʿism*, especially chapter 2, "The Pre-Existence of the Imam," pp. 29–59, and chapter 4, "The Super-Existence of the Imam," pp. 99–123. For a comparative study between Imamology and Christology, see: Amir-Moezzi, "Alī et le Coran (aspects de l'imamologie duodécimaine XIV)," *Revue des Sciences Philosophiques et Théologiques* 98 (2014), pp. 696–703.

30. The excessive use of drones shows that technological development does not mean avoiding civilian victims. On the contrary, the so-called "smart" weapons and "surgical" attacks kill many innocent people. Akbar Ahmed explains and documents the use of these weapons in Afghanistan, Pakistan, and Yemen. See Akbar Ahmed, *The Thistle and the Drone: How America's War on Terror Became a Global War on Tribal Islam*, Brookings Institution Press, Washington, 2013.

31. See Khan Abdul Ghaffar Khan's autobiography, *My Life and Struggle: Autobiography of Badshah Khan*, H. Bouman (tr.), Hind Pocket Books, Delhi, 1969. See also: Mukulika Banerjee, *The Pathan Unarmed: Opposition & Memory in the North West Frontier*, School of American Research Press, Oxford University Press, Karachi, 2000. The young Pakistani Malala Yousafzai, Nobel Peace Prize winner, could be considered the spiritual daughter of Bacha Khan. She is from the same ethnicity and tribal zone.

32. See Maulana Abul Kalam Azad's autobiography, *India Wins Freedom: An Autobiographical Narrative*, Orient Longman, Hyderabad, 1988.

33. See, for instance: Asghar Ali Engineer, *The Prophet of Non-Violence, Spirit of Peace, Compassion and Universality in Islam*, Vitasta Publishing, New Delhi, 2011.

34. Mahmoud Mohammed Taha, *The Second Message of Islam*, A. An-Naʿim (tr.), Syracuse University Press, Syracuse, NY, 1987; Edward Thomas, *Islam's Perfect*

Stranger: The Life of Mahmud Muhammad Taha, Muslim Reformer of Sudan, I. B. Tauris, London, 2010; and Mohamed A. Mahmoud, *Quest for Divinity: A Critical Examination of the Thought of Mahmud Muhammad Taha*, Syracuse University Press, Syracuse, NY, 2006.

35. See: Jawdat Said, *Vie islamiche alla nonviolenza*, P. Pizzi (tr.), Zikkaron, Marzabotto, 2017; and Jean-Marie Muller, "Visite à Jawdat Saïd," *Désarmer les dieux: le christianisme et l'islam au regard de l'exigence de non-violence*, Le Relié, Gordes, 2009, pp. 562–577. Among the Syrian disciples of Jawdat Said are Khalis Jalabi and Afra Jalabi. The Iraqi thinker Abdul Hussain Shaban is vice president of the Academic University for Non-Violence (AUNOHR) in Beirut.

36. See: Ramin Jahanbegloo, *Introduction to Nonviolence*, Palgrave Macmillan, New York, 2014; and *The Gandhian Moment*, Harvard University Press, London, 2013.

37. See: Mohammed Abu-Nimer, *Nonviolence and Peace Building in Islam: Theory and Practice*, University Press of Florida, Gainesville, 2003. See also: Marcia Hermansen, "Muslim Theologians of Nonviolence," in *Religion and Violence: Muslim and Christian Theological and Pedagogical Reflections*, E. Aslan and M. Hermansen (eds.), Wiener Beiträge zur Islamforschung, Springer, Wiesbaden, 2017, pp. 147–162.

38. *Apostolic Exhortation Evangelii Gaudium*, paragraph 253, promulgated in November 24, 2013, http://www.vatican.va/content/francesco/en/apost_exhortations/documents/papa-francesco_esortazione-ap_20131124_evangelii-gaudium.html.

39. Girard, *Battling to the End*, p. 209.

40. Ibid., p. 211.

41. Ibid., p. 215.

42. Ibid., p. 214.

43. Thomas Scheffler, "Islam and Islamism in the Mirror of Girard's Mimetic Theory," p. 131.

44. Thomas Scheffler, "Islam and Islamism in the Mirror of Girard's Mimetic Theory," p. 131. Olivier Roy, *Jihad and Death: The Global Appeal of the Islamic State*, C. Schoch (tr.), Oxford University Press, New York, 2017, p. 6.

45. Girard, *Battling to the End*, p. 214.

46. See: Gowhar Quadir Wani, "Understanding Peace and Nonviolence in Islam with Maulānā Wahīduddīn Khān," *Journal of Islamic Thought and Civilization*, vol. 7, no. 2 (2017), pp. 52–61. See also: Irfan A. Omar, "Towards an Islamic Theology of Nonviolence: A Critical Appraisal of Maulana Wahiduddin Khan's View of Jihad," *Vidyajyoti Journal of Theological Reflection*, (Part I), vol. 72, no. 9 (2008), pp. 671–680; (Part II), vol. 72, no. 10 (2008), pp. 751–758.

47. Maulana Wahiduddin Khan, *Non-Violence and Islam*, Goodword Books, New Delhi, 2013, p. 3.

Bibliography

Abdel Haleem, M. A. S., *The Qur'an*, Oxford University Press, Oxford, 2004.

Abdel Razek, Ali, *Islam and the Foundations of Political Power*, M. Loutfi (tr.), A. Filali-Ansary (ed.), Edinburgh University Press, The Aga Khan University, Edinburgh, 2012.

Abū Dāwūd, *Sunan Abū Dāwūd*, Sayyid Muḥammad Sayyid, ʿAbd al-Qādir ʿAbd al-Khayr, Sayyid Ibrāhīm, eds., Dār al-Ḥadīth, Cairo, 2010.

Abu-Nimer, Mohammed, *Nonviolence and Peace Building in Islam: Theory and Practice*, University Press of Florida, Gainesville, 2003.

Abusulayman, Abdulhamid (ed.), *Islamization of Knowledge: General Principles and Work Plan*, The International Institute of Islamic Thought (IIIT), Herndon, VA, 3rd ed. 1997.

Afsaruddin, Asma, *Striving in the Path of God: Jihād and Martyrdom in Islamic Thought*, Oxford University Press, New York, 2013.

Ahmed, Akbar, *The Thistle and the Drone: How America's War on Terror Became a Global War on Tribal Islam*, Brookings Institution Press, Washington, DC, 2013.

Ahmed, Waleed, "Lot's Daughters in the Qurʾān: An Investigation Through the Lens of Intertextuality," in *New Perspectives on the Qurʾān: The Qurʾān in its Historical Context 2*, Gabriel S. Reynolds (ed.), Routledge, Abingdon, 2011, pp. 411–424.

Akyol, Mustafa, *The Islamic Jesus: How the King of the Jews Became a Prophet of the Muslims*, St Martin's Press, New York, 2017.

Alalwani, Taha Jabir, *Apostasy in Islam: A Historical and Scriptural Analysis*, N. Roberts (tr.), IIIT, London, 2011.

Albānī (al-), *Silsilat al-aḥādīth al-ḍaʿīfa wa al-mawḍūʿa*, Maktabat al-maʿārif, Riyad, 1992.

Amir-Moezzi, Mohammad Ali, "Alī et le Coran (aspects de l'imamologie duodécimaine XIV)," *Revue des Sciences Philosophiques et Théologiques* 98 (2014), pp. 696–703.

———, *The Divine Guide in Early Shiʿism: The Sources of Esotericism in Islam*, D. Streight (tr.), State University of New York Press, Albany, 1994.

Amir-Moezzi, Mohammad Ali, and Guillaume Dye (eds.), *Le Coran des Historiens*, Cerf, Paris, 2019.

Arafat, Walid, "New Light on the Story of Banū Qurayẓa and the Jews of Medina," *Journal of the Royal Asiatic Society of Great Britain and Ireland* (1976), pp. 100–107.

Ayada, Souad, *L'islam des théophanies, une religion à l'épreuve de l'art*, CNRS Editions, Paris, 2010.

Ayoub, Mahmoud, *A Muslim View of Christianity: Essays on Dialogue*, Irfan A. Omar (ed.), Orbis Books, New York, 2007.

Azad, Maulana Abul Kalam, *India Wins Freedom: An Autobiographical Narrative*, Orient Longman, Hyderabad, 1988.

Banerjee, Mukulika, *The Pathan Unarmed: Opposition & Memory in the North West Frontier*, School of American Research Press, Oxford University Press, Karachi, 2000.

Bayhaqī (al-), *al-Sunan al-Kubrā*, I. M. ʿAbd al-Ḥamīd (ed.), Dār al-Ḥadīth, Cairo, 2008.

Bennabi, Malek, *Les Conditions de la Renaissance*, Editions ANEP, Alger, 2005.

Bukhārī (al-), *al-Tārīkh al-Kabīr*, Dāʾirat al-maʿārif al-ʿuthmāniyya, ʿAbd al-Muʿīd Khān (ed.), Hyderabad Deccan, 1941–1959.

Chodkiewicz, Michel, *An Ocean Without Shore: Ibn ʿArabi, the Book, and the Law*, State University of New York Press, Albany, 1993.

Clohessy, Christopher Paul, *Half of My Heart: The Narratives of Zaynab, Daughter of ʿAlî*, Gorgias Press, Piscataway, 2018.

Cuypers, Michel, *The Composition of the Qurʾān: Rhetorical Analysis*, Bloomsbury, London, 2016.

Dall'Oglio, Paolo, *Innamorato dell'Islam, credente in Gesù, dell'islamofilia*, Jaca Book, Milan, 2nd ed. 2013.

———, *Speranza nell'Islam: Interpretazione della prospettiva escatologica di Corano XVIII*, Marietti, Genova, 1991.

De Chergé, Christian, *L'Autre que nous attendons, homélies de père Christian de Chergé, 1970–1996* (Editions de Bellefontaine, 2006). An Italian extract published on the Vatican website, accessed March 25, 2019. https://w2.vatican.va/content/osservatore-romano/it/comments/2010/documents/299q01b1.html.

De Tanoüarn, G., and L. Lineul, "Entretien avec René Girard," *La nouvelle revue Certitudes* 16 (2003), pp. 35–50.

Draz, M. A., *Introduction to the Qur'ān*, I. B. Tauris, London, 2000.

Dupuis, Jacques, *Toward a Christian Theology of Religious Pluralism*, Orbis Books, New York, 1997.

Engineer, Asghar Ali, *Islam and Liberation Theology: Essays on Liberative Elements in Islam*, Sterling Publishers, New Delhi, 1990.

———, *The Prophet of Non-Violence, Spirit of Peace, Compassion and Universality in Islam*, Vitasta Publishing, New Delhi, 2011.

Esack, Farid, "Lot and His Offer: 2016 IQSA Presidential Address," *Journal of International Qur'ānic Studies Association JIQSA* 2 (2017), pp. 7–33.

———, *Qur'ān Liberation & Pluralism: An Islamic Perspective of Interreligious Solidarity against Oppression*, Oneworld, Oxford, 1997.

Faizer, Rizwi S., "Muḥammad and the Medinan Jews: A Comparison of the Texts of Ibn Isḥāq's Kitāb Sīrat Rasūl Allāh with al-Wāqidī's Kitāb al-Maghāzī," *International Journal of Middle East Studies* 28 (1996), pp. 463–489.

Francis, Pope, *Apostolic Exhortation Evangelii Gaudium*, November 24, 2013, accessed March 20, 2019. http://www.vatican.va/content/francesco/en/apost_exhortations/documents/papa-francesco_esortazione-ap_20131124_evangelii-gaudium.html.

Gilliot, Claude, "Narratives," *Encyclopaedia of the Qur'ān*, Jane Dammen McAuliffe (ed.), Brill, Leiden, 2003.

Girard, René, *Battling to the End: Conversations with Benoît Chantre*, Mary Baker (tr.), Michigan State University Press, East Lansing, 2010.

———, "Entretien avec René Girard," propos recueillis par G. De Tanoüarn et L. Lineul, *La nouvelle revue Certitudes* 16 (2003), pp. 35–50.

———, *I See Satan Fall Like Lightning*, James G. Williams (tr.), Orbis Books, Maryknoll, New York, 2001.

———, *The One by Whom Scandal Comes*, M. B. DeBevoise (tr.), Michigan State University Press, East Lansing, 2014.

———, *Things Hidden since the Foundation of the World*, in collaboration with Jean-Michel Oughourlian and Guy Lefort, S. Bann and M. Metteer (tr.), Stanford University Press, Redwood City, 1987.

Gonzales, Valérie, *Beauty and Islam: Aesthetics in Islamic Art and Architecture*, The Institute of Ismaili Studies, I. B. Tauris, London, 2001.

———, *Le Piège de Salomon: La Pensée de l'art dans le Coran*, Albin Michel, Paris, 2002.

Goodhart, Sandor, "Fathers and Sons, Sacrifice and Substitution: Mimetic Theory and Islam in Genesis 22 and Sura 37," *Mimetic Theory and Islam*, pp. 65–85.

Goudie, Kenneth A., *Reinventing Jihād: Jihād Ideology from the Conquest of Jerusalem to the End of the Ayyūbids (c. 492/1099–647/1249)*, Brill, Leiden, 2019.

Guenon, René, *The Crisis of the Modern World*, M. Pallis, A. Osborne, R. C. Nicholson (tr.), Sophia Perennis, Revised Edition, Hillsdale NY, 2004.

———, *The Reign of Quantity and the Signs of the Times*, Sophia Perennis, Hillsdale NY, 2004.

Hachem, Constance Arminjon, *Chiisme et état: Les clercs à l'épreuve de la modernité*, CNRS Éditions, Paris, 2013.

Hallāj (al-), al-Ḥusayn Ibn Manṣūr, *Il Cristo dell'Islam, scritti mistici [Ṭawāsīn]*, A. Ventura (tr.), Mondadori, Milan, 2007.

Hermansen, Marcia, "Muslim Theologians of Nonviolence," in *Religion and Violence: Muslim and Christian Theological and Pedagogical Reflections*, E. Aslan and M. Hermansen (eds.), Wiener Beiträge zur Islamforschung, Springer, Wiesbaden, 2017, pp. 147–162.

Ibn al-Ḥakam, *Futūḥ ifrīqiyya wa al-andalus*, A. al-Ṭabbāʿ (ed.), Dār al-kitāb al-lubnānī, Beirut, 1964.

Ibn al-Nadīm, *al-Fihrist*, Reza Tajaddod (ed.), printed by the editor, Tehran, 1971.

Ibn Isḥāq, *The Life of Muḥammad: A Translation of Ibn Isḥāq's Sīrat Rasūl Allāh*, A. Guillaume (tr.), Oxford University Press, Karachi, 1982.

Ibn Kathīr, *al-Bidāya wa al-Nihāya*, Maktabat al-maʿārif, Beirut, 1991.

Ibn Māja, *Sunan Ibn Māja*, ʿAbd al-Bāqī and al-Dhahabī (eds.), Dār al-Ḥadīth, Cairo, 2010.

Iqbal, Muhammad, *The Reconstruction of Religious Thought in Islam*, M. Saeed Sheikh (ed.), Stanford University Press, Iqbal Academy Pakistan, Redwood City, 2013.

Itani, Talal, *Quran in English, Modern English Translation*, www.tanzil.net.

Izutsu, Toshihiko, *Sufism and Taoism: A Comparative Study of Key Philosophical Concepts*, University of California Press, Berkeley, 1983.

Jahanbegloo, Ramin, *The Gandhian Moment*, Harvard University Press, London, 2013.

———, *Introduction to Nonviolence*, Palgrave Macmillan, New York, 2014.

John Paul II, Pope, Encyclical Letter: *Fides et Ratio* (1998), accessed March 20, 2019. http://w2.vatican.va/content/john-paul-ii/en/encyclicals/documents/hf_jp-ii_enc_14091998_fides-et-ratio.html.

Juynboll, G. H. A., *Encyclopedia of Canonical Ḥadīth*, Brill, Leiden, 2007.

Kermani, Navid, *Incroyable christianisme*, R. Kremer (tr.), Salvator, Paris, 2016.

Khan, Khan Abdul Ghaffar, *My Life and Struggle: Autobiography of Badshah Khan*, H. Bouman (tr.), Hind Pocket Books, Delhi, 1969.

Khan, Maulana Wahiduddin, *Non-Violence and Islam*, Goodword Books, New Delhi, 2013.

Kirazli, Sadik, "Re-Examining the Story of the Banū Qurayẓah Jews in Medina with Reference to the Account of Ibn Isḥāq," *Australian Journal of Islamic Studies* 4, no. 1 (2019), pp. 1–17.

Kugle, Scott Siraj al-Haqq, *Homosexuality in Islam: Critical Reflection on Gay, Lesbian, and Transgender Muslims*, Oneworld, Oxford, 2010.

Lagarde, François, *René Girard ou la Christianisation des Sciences Humaines*, Peter Lang, New York, 1994.

Laoust, Henri, "Aḥmad b. Ḥanbal," *Encyclopaedia of Islam, Second Edition*, accessed April 3, 2021, https://referenceworks.brillonline.com/browse/encyclopaedia-of-islam-2.

Lassner, Jacob, *Demonizing the Queen of Sheba: Boundaries of Gender and Culture in Postbiblical Judaism and Medieval Islam*, University of Chicago Press, Chicago, 1993.

Lawson, Todd, *The Crucifixion and the Qur'ān: A Study in the History of Muslim Thought*, Oneworld Publications, Oxford, 2009.

Lecker, Michael, *The "Constitution of Medina": Muḥammad's First Legal Document*, The Darwin Press, Princeton, 2004.

Lings, Martin, *Muḥammad: His Life Based on the Earliest Sources*, Inner Traditions, Rochester, VT, 2006.

Maʿmar Ibn Rāshid, *The Expeditions: An Early Biography of Muḥammad, According to the Recension of ʿAbd al-Razzāq al-Ṣanʿānī*, Sean W. Anthony (tr.), New York University Press, New York, 2015.

Mahmoud, Mohamed A., *Quest for Divinity: A Critical Examination of the Thought of Mahmud Muhammad Taha*, Syracuse University Press, Syracuse, NY, 2006.

Mālik b. Anas, *al-Muwaṭṭa'*, M. Fadel and Monette (tr.), Harvard University Press, Cambridge, MA, 2019.

Mokrani, Adnane, "ʿĀshūrā' in Sunnite Mirrors: Confused Borders between Joy and Sadness," *Islamochristiana* 36 (2010), pp. 47–62.

———, *Naqd al-adyān ʿinda Ibn Ḥazm al-andalusī*, IIIT, Herndon, VA, 2008.

Muller, Jean-Marie, *Désarmer les dieux: le christianisme et l'islam au regard de l'exigence de non-violence*, Le Relié, Gordes, 2009.

Muslim, *Ṣaḥīḥ Muslim, English Translation*, Nasiruddin al-Khattab (tr.), Huda Khattab (ed.), Darussalam, Riyadh, 2007.

Nasr, Seyyed Hossein, and Ramin Jahanbegloo, *In Search of the Sacred: A Conversation with Seyyed Hossein Nasr on His Life and Thought*, Praeger, Santa Barbara, CA, 2010.

Nasr, Seyyed Vali Reza, "Islamization of Knowledge: A Critical Overview," *Islamic Studies* 30, no. 3 (1991), pp. 387–400.

Nawawī (al-), *Riyāḍ al-Ṣāliḥīn: A Translation and Commentary*, Moulana Afzal Ismail (ed.), Muslims at Work Publications, Heidelberg (South Africa), 2nd ed. 2016.

Nurbakhsh, Javad, *Traditions of the Prophet*, Khaniqahi Nimatullahi Publications, New York, 1981.

Omar, Irfan A., "Towards an Islamic Theology of Nonviolence: A Critical Appraisal of Maulana Wahiduddin Khan's View of Jihad," *Vidyajyoti Journal of Theological Reflection*

(Part I), vol. 72, no. 9 (2008), pp. 671–680; (Part II), vol. 72, no. 10 (2008), pp. 751–758.

Palaver, Wolfgang, *Transforming the Sacred into Saintliness: Reflecting on Violence and Religion with René Girard*, Cambridge University Press, Cambridge, 2020.

Qurṭubī (al-), *Tafsīr al-Qurṭubī*, S. M. al-Badrī (ed.), Dār al-kutub al-ʿilmiyya, Beirut, 4th ed. 2014.

Qushayrī (al-), *Tafsīr al-Qushayrī al-musammā Laṭāʾif al-ishārāt*, ʿAbd al-Laṭīf Ḥasan ʿAbd al-Raḥmān (ed.), Dār al-kutub al-ʿilmiyya, Beirut, 3rd ed. 2015.

Qutb, Sayyid, *Milestones*, A. B. al-Mehri (ed.), Maktabah Booksellers and Publishers, Birmingham, 2006.

Rāzī, Fakhr al-Dīn, *Tafsīr al-Rāzī, al-Tafsīr al-kabīr aw Mafātīḥ al-ghayb*, Dār al-Fikr, Beirut, 1981.

Roy, Olivier, *Jihad and Death: The Global Appeal of the Islamic State*, C. Schoch (tr.), Oxford University Press, New York, 2017.

Rūmī, *Dīvān-e Shams, Ghazaliyyāt*, Ghazal (ode) 207, accessed April 6, 2021. https://ganjoor.net/moulavi/shams/ghazalsh/sh207/.

Rūmī, Jalāl al-Dīn, *The Mathnawi*, R. A. Nicholson (tr.), Cambridge University Press, London, 1930.

Ruspoli, Stéphane, *Le traité de l'Esprit saint de Rûzbehân de Shîrâz*, Cerf, Paris, 2001.

Said, Jawdat, *Lā ikrāh fī al-dīn, dirāsāt wa abḥāth fī al-fikr al-islāmī [No Compulsion in Religion, Studies in Islamic Thought]*, M. Nafīsa (ed.), Al-ʿilm wa al-salām lil-dirāsāt wa al-nashr, Damascus, 1997.

———, *Vie islamiche alla nonviolenza*, P. Pizzi (tr.), Zikkaron, Marzabotto, 2017.

Schacht, Joseph, "Abū Ḥanīfa al-Nuʿmān," *Encyclopaedia of Islam, Second Edition*, accessed April 3, 2021, https://referenceworks.brillonline.com/browse/encyclopaedia-of-islam-2.

———, "al-Awzāʿī," *Encyclopaedia of Islam, Second Edition*, accessed April 3, 2021, https://referenceworks.brillonline.com/browse/encyclopaedia-of-islam-2.

———, "Mālik b. Anas," *Encyclopaedia of Islam, Second Edition*, accessed April 3, 2021, https://referenceworks.brillonline.com/browse/encyclopaedia-of-islam-2.

Scheffler, Thomas, "Islam and Islamism in the Mirror of Girard's Mimetic Theory," in *Mimetic Theory and Islam: "The Wound Where Light Enters,"* M. Kirwan and A. Achtar (eds.), Palgrave Macmillan, New York, 2019, pp. 129–140.

Scubla, Lucien, *Lire Lévi-Strauss*, Odile Jacob, Paris, 1998.

Sulamī (al-), *Tafsīr al-Sulamī aw Ḥaqāʾq al-tafsīr, tafsīr al-Qurʾān al-ʿazīz*, Sayyid ʿImrān (ed.), Dār al-kutub al-ʿilmiyya, Beirut, 2nd ed. 2016.

Suyūṭī (al-), *Le parfait manuel des sciences coraniques al-Itqān fī ʿulūm al-Qurʾān*, Michel Lagarde (tr.), Brill, Leiden, 2018.

Ṭabarī (al-), *Tafsīr al-Ṭabarī, Jāmiʿ al-bayān ʿan taʾwīl āy al-Qurʾān*, ʿAbd Allāh bin ʿAbd al-Muḥsin al-Turkī (ed.), Hajr lil-ṭibāʿa wa al-nashr, al-Jīza, Cairo, 2001.

———, *The History of al-Ṭabarī, vol. XII, the Battle of al-Qādisiyya and the Conquest of Syria and Palestine*, Yohanan Friedmann (tr.), State University of New York Press, Albany, 1992.

Tabrīzī (al-) al-Khaṭīb, *Mishkāt al-Maṣābīḥ*, al-Albani (ed.), al-Maktab al-Islāmī, Beirut, 2nd ed. 1979.

Taha, Mahmoud Mohammed, *The Second Message of Islam*, A. An-Naʿim (tr.), Syracuse University Press, Syracuse, NY, 1987.

Thomas, Edward, *Islam's Perfect Stranger: The Life of Mahmud Muhammad Taha, Muslim Reformer of Sudan*, I. B. Tauris, London, 2010.

Tirmidhī (al-), *Sunan al-Tirmidhī*, M. M. H. al-Dhahabī (ed.), Dār al-Ḥadīth, Cairo, 2010.

Wani, Gowhar Quadir, "Understanding Peace and Nonviolence in Islam with Maulānā Wahīduddīn Khān," *Journal of Islamic Thought and Civilization* 7, no. 2 (2017), pp. 52–61.

Wiederhold, Lutz, "Shatm," *Encyclopaedia of Islam, Second Edition*, accessed June 4, 2021, https://referenceworks.brillonline.com/browse/encyclopaedia-of-islam-2.

Yusuf, Imtiyaz (ed.), *Islam and Knowledge: Al Faruqi's Concept of Religion in Islamic Thought*, I. B. Tauris, London, 2012.

Index

Abbasids, 81, 85; caliphs, 74; revolution, 85
Abraham (Ibrāhīm), 34, 53–55, 57, 61, 62, 101 (n. 25); sacrifice, xi, 5, 52, 53, 57, 58, 100 (n. 9); Abrahamic religions, 3, 4, 6, 10, 28, 60; Abrahamic revolution, xi
Abū Bakr, 78
Abū Ḥanīfa, 81
Abu-Nimer, Mohammed, 89
Adam, 12, 19, 44, 46–48, 51, 99 (n. 3), 100 (n. 9); children of, 49; two sons of, 14, 19, 49, 51, 58, 60, 63, 71
ahimsa, 88
Aḥmad Ibn Ḥanbal, 81, 103 (n. 3)
Algerians, 87; Algerian War of Independence, 87
ʿAlī Ibn Abī Ṭālib, 83, 84
all-against-one, 82, 89, 91
Amir-Moezzi, Mohammad Ali, 84
ʿAmr Ibn al-ʿĀṣ, 79
angel, 44–46, 48, 49, 56, 61, 84. *See also* Gabriel
Antichrist, 17, 18. *See also* Dajjāl
apostasy, 39, 40, 98 (n. 67)
ʿAqīqa, 57
Arabs, 76, 103 (n. 6); Arab Spring, 89; Arabian Peninsula, 75–77
archaic religion, ix, xi, xx, xxi
associationism. See *shirk*
ʿAṭṭār, 99 (n. 3)
Augustine, x
Azad, Abul Kalam, xiv, 89

Bacha Khan, 105 (n. 31). *See also* Khan, Abdul Ghaffar
Banū Qurayẓa, xiii, 77, 78, 83, 103 (n. 10)
Belgium, 87
Bennabi, Malek, 1, 94 (n. 6)
Bible, xx, xxi, 3, 6, 7, 9, 50, 54, 61, 62, 100 (n. 9); Hebrew Bible, xix, xxi, 6, 7, 8, 10, 28
Bilqīs, 101 (n. 23), 102 (n. 31). *See also* Queen of Sheba.
blasphemy, 30, 39, 40, 62
Buddhism, x

Byzantines, 75, 78; Byzantium, 74; empire, 74

Cain and Abel, 40, 47, 60, 63. *See also* Adam: two sons of
Children of Israel, 19, 40, 49
Christianity, ix–xii, xiv, xix–xxi, 2, 4–6, 8, 28, 90, 93 (n. 2); Christian–Muslim dialogue, xi, xii; Christianization of knowledge, 1; Christians, xiv, 18, 28, 31, 51, 95 (n. 17)
colonialism, 87, 88; colonial powers, 42; colonial rule, 86
Commandments, 9–11; Mosaic Commandments, 10; Ten Commandments, 65. *See also* Decalogue.
Companions, 9, 12, 37, 73, 75, 76, 79, 103 (n. 3). See also *Ṣaḥāba*.
Congo, 87
Constantinople, 74, 102 (n. 2)
consultation, xiii, 36, 37, 60, 67, 79. See also *shūrā*
Cross, xii, xix, 20, 29, 30, 32, 33, 63; Crucifixion, xii, 29, 30, 95 (n. 17), 97 (n. 53)

Dajjāl (al-), 17. *See also* Antichrist
Dall'Oglio, Paolo, 100 (n. 9)
Damascus, 83
Dante, x
David, 51, 52, 66, 67
De Chergé, Christian, 33
Decalogue, 9, 10. *See also* Commandments
Draz, Muhammad Abdullah, 10

Egypt, 78
Engineer, Asghar Ali, xiv, 89
Esack, Farid, 61
escalation, xx, 4, 37, 90, 91
Eve, 12, 19, 47
exclusivism, 27, 28, 35, 50
Exile, 8

Fakh, 81
Fārūqī, Ismāʿīl Rājī al-, 1, 90 (n. 2)
Fāṭima, 57, 83
Fitna, 12, 13, 30, 79. *See also* scandal

Gabriel, 84
Gandhi, x, xiv, 88, 89; Gandhian moment, xiv, 42, 88
Ghassanids, 75
Ghazālī (al-), 99 (n 3)
Girard, René, ix–xi, xiii, xiv, xix, xx, xxii, 1–4, 6–10, 12–14, 16, 17, 19, 20, 23, 27, 28, 29, 30, 32–34, 57, 62, 82, 90, 93 (n. 2), 94 (n. 8), 95 (n. 17), 104 (n. 22)
golden calf, 15, 31
Gospel, xx, 10, 19. *See also* New Testament
Green Wave, 89
Guenon, René, 1, 94 (n. 4)

Hagar, 54, 56, 57
Ḥallāj, 81, 99 (n. 3)
Hāmān, 8
Hinduism, x, 88
Hiroshima and Nagasaki, 87
Holocaust, 87
holocaust, 5, 6
Ḥudaybiya, 75, 76, 83
Ḥusayn, 9, 83–85, 105 (n. 28)

Ibn ʿArabī, 26, 96 (n. 42)
Ifrīqiyya, 79, 104 (n. 14)
Iqbal, Muhammad, 5, 95 (n. 13)
Isaac, 53, 54
Ishmael (Ismāʿīl), 54–57
Islam, ix-xiv, xx-xxii, 2, 4–6, 12, 18, 22, 25, 33, 34, 40, 54, 58, 73, 76, 78, 80, 81, 84, 89, 90, 96 (n. 37), 104 (n.

17, 22), 105 (n. 28); *islām*, 33, 35, 59; homeland of, 82; Islamism, x, 90, 104 (n. 22); Islamist terrorism, 82, 90; Islamist radicalism, xx; Islamization of knowledge, 1, 90 (n. 2); Islamization of radicalism, 90. *See also* Muslims

Jahanbegloo, Ramin, xiii, 89
Jainism, xiv, 88
Jesus, xii, xiv, xix, xx, 10, 13, 17–20, 29, 32–35, 63, 95 (n. 17), 97 (n. 54); Christ, xiv, xix, 4, 21, 28, 29, 32; forsaken, 33
Jews, 28, 39, 51, 87, 95 (n. 25); *See* Banū Qurayẓa; Children of Israel; Judaism
Jihad, 81, 82; *jihād*, 82; jihadism, xiii; jihadist movements, 81; jihadist theory, 74, 79–81, 103 (n. 5)
jizya, 80. *See also* poll tax
Job, 101 (n. 26)
John the Baptist, 21
Jordan, 75
Joseph, xiii, 7, 9, 15, 58–60, 71
Judaism, xi, xix, 2, 5, 54

Kalām, 43, 63
Karbalā', 81, 83, 84, 105 (n. 28)
Khālid Ibn al-Walīd, 78, 104 (n. 13)
Khan, Abdul Ghaffar, xiv, 89, 105 (n. 31). *See also* Bacha Khan
Khan, Wahiduddin, xiv, 91
Khiḍr, Khaḍir, 63
King, Martin Luther, Jr., 89
Kūfa, 83, 84

Lot, 60–62

Mahdī (al-), 9, 84. *See also* Qā'im
Mālik Ibn Anas, 81
Mandela, Nelson, 89
Mary, 29, 64, 101 (n. 23)
Mecca (Makkah), 55, 56, 62, 76, 77, 83, 103 (n. 10)
Medina, 9, 75–77, 79, 83, 95 (n. 25), 103 (n. 12); Constitution of, 77. *See also* Yathrib
Mehmet I, the Conqueror, 74
mimetism, 27, 29, 32, 35, 51, 85; mimetic cycle, 7–9; mimetic desire, x, 3, 4, 20, 22, 35; mimetic theory, ix–xi, xiii, xix–xxii, 1, 9, 91
Moses, xiii, 4, 19, 31, 63–65, 95 (n. 25)
Muḥammad, 5, 6, 9, 12, 17, 22, 31, 33–36, 38, 40, 62, 73, 77, 79, 83, 84, 99 (n. 5)
Muslims, x, xiii, xiv, 18, 30, 31, 33, 37, 51, 57, 74–79, 81, 89, 94 (n. 2), 95 (n. 25), 98 (n. 75), 105 (n. 28)
Mu'ta, 75, 78, 104 (n. 13)
myth, xix, 2, 6, 7, 28, 43, 75; mythology, xix, 8, 29, 32, 95 (n. 17)

Nasr, Seyyed Hossein, 1, 94 (n. 5)
New Testament, xix, xxi, 8, 29, 32. *See also* Gospel
North Africa, 78–79

Ottoman caliphate, 99 (n. 75); empire, 74; expansions, 74

Persia, 80; Persians, 85. *See also* Sassanid Empire
Pharaoh, 8, 18, 19, 62, 95 (n. 25)
pluralism, 26, 28, 29, 60, 85; theology of religious, xxii, 28
poll tax, 80, 104 (n. 17). See also *jizya*
Promised Land, 8
prophecy, 4, 35, 51, 63, 74, 102 (n. 31); prophethood, 3, 98 (n. 75)

Qādisiyya (al-), 80
Qā'im (al-). *See* Mahdī

Queen of Sheba, 63, 66–71, 101 (n. 23), 102 (n. 29, 31). *See also* Bilqīs
Quraysh, 75–77, 83, 103 (n. 6, 7, 10)
Qutb, Sayyid, 81, 82, 104 (n. 19, 20)

relativism, xx, 28, 29
resurrection, xii, 6, 8, 9, 30, 31, 83, 84, 90; of Jesus, 8, 31–33, 95 (n. 17), Day of, 27, 28
Rib'ī Ibn 'Āmir, 80–82, 104 (n. 19, 20)
Roy, Olivier, 90
Rūmī, 26, 99 (n. 3)
Rūzbihān Baqlī, 99 (n. 3)

sacrifice, xi, xxi, 2, 3, 5, 6, 49, 50, 52–58, 62, 68, 88, 93 (n. 2), 99 (n. 5), 100 (n. 9); post-sacrificial religion, xi, 58; sacrificial religion, 2, 3, 30. *See also* Abraham: sacrifice
Ṣaḥāba, 73. *See also* Companions
Said, Jawdat, 37, 106 (n. 35)
Salafism, 105 (n. 28)
Salmān the Persian, 83
Sarah, 54, 57, 62
Sassanid Empire, 79
Satan, 2, 12–20, 29, 33, 39, 46, 47, 50, 52, 55, 57, 64, 70
satyagraha, xiv, 88
Saudi Arabia, 75
scandal, xix, 12, 13, 16, 17, 30, 47, 61, 64, 81, 86. See also *fitna*
scapegoat, ix, xix, 7, 18, 79, 85
Scheffler, Thomas, xx, 90
Scheler, Max, x
Shi'i Tradition, 84, 85; Shiism, 9, 99 (n. 75)
shirk, 22, 60
shūrā, 37. *See also* consultation
Sīra, 33, 73, 75; *al-Siyar wa al-Maghāzī*, 74, 75
slavery, 8, 48, 80, 86
Solomon, 63, 66–71, 101 (n. 26)
South Africa, xiv
Successors, *Tābi'ūn*, 73; Successors (caliphs), 74; Successors of the Successors, *Tābi'ū al-tābi'īn*, 73
Sufis, 43, 54, 63, 96 (n. 46); Sufi tradition, 49; Sufism, xii, 25–26, 81
Suhrawardī, 81
Sulamī (al-), 31
Sunna, 17, 33–35, 73; *sunna ḥasana*, 52, 99 (n. 4); *sunna sayyi'a*, 52, 99 (n. 4); Sunni Tradition, 105 (n. 28); Sunnis, 105 (n. 28); Sunnism, 105 (n. 28)

Tabūk, 75
Taha, Mahmoud Mohammed, 89
tawḥīd, 22, 25, 59, 60
terrorism, 80, 82, 89–91; attacks, ix, xx; groups, 82
Thomas Aquinas, x
Tunisia, 89, 104 (n. 14)
Tutu, Desmond, 89

'Ubayd Allāh Ibn Ziyād, 83
Uḥud, 78
'Umar Ibn al-Khaṭṭāb, 78
Umayyads, 74, 81, 83, 85, 105 (n. 28); empire, 79
Usāma Ibn Zayd, 78

Vedānta, x
Vietnam War, 87

World War I, 86; World War II, 86–87

Yathrib, 83. *See also* Medina

Zaynab, 57, 83
Zoroastrianism, 10